THE BALKAN WARS
1912-1913

Jacob Gould Schurman

Contents

PREFACE 7
INTRODUCTION 12
I TURKEY AND THE BALKAN STATES 22
THE TURKISH EMPIRE IN EUROPE 22
THE EARLIER SLAV EMPIRES 24
TURKISH OPPRESSION OF SLAVS 26
GREEK ECCLESIASTICAL DOMINATION OF SLAV 27
SERVIAN INDEPENDENCE 29
GREEK INDEPENDENCE 29
BULGARIAN INDEPENDENCE 30
THE BALKAN COUNTRIES 32
CAUSES OF THE FIRST BALKAN WAR 33
THE BALKAN LEAGUE 34
GREECE AND THE LEAGUE 35
GREEK AND BULGARIAN ANTIPATHIES 37
THE CRETAN PROBLEM 38
MR. VENIZELOS'S SOLUTION 39
THE WAR 40
GREEK MILITARY AND NAVAL OPERATIONS 41
SERB MILITARY OPERATIONS 42
BULGARIAN MILITARY OPERATIONS 43
THE COLLAPSE OF TURKEY 43
II THE WAR BETWEEN THE ALLIES 46
RIVAL AMBITIONS OF THE ALLIES 46
ALBANIA A CAUSE OF FRICTION 48
RECOIL OF SERVIA TOWARD THE AEGEAN 49
TREATY RESTRICTIONS 50
THE APPLE OF DISCORD 50
THE CLAIM OF BULGARIA 52
RACIAL PROPAGANDA IN MACEDONIA 53
RACIAL FACTS AND FALLACIES 54
PERSONAL OBSERVATIONS AND EXPERIENCES 56
THE ATTITUDE OF SERVIA 58
PROPOSED REVISION OF TREATY AND ARBITRATION 59
DELAY AND OPPOSITION OF BULGARIA 60
BULGARIA'S UNCOMPROMISING POLICY 61
THE CONCILIATORY SPIRIT OF GREECE 62
BULGARIA BEGINS HOSTILITIES 64
TERMS OF PEACE 65
THE ATTITUDE OF ROUMANIA 66
THE WORK AND REWARD OF MONTENEGRO 68
THE PROBLEM OF ALBANIA 69
THE AEGEAN ISLANDS AND CRETE 70
KING CONSTANTINE 71
COST OF THE WAR 71
THE FUTURE OF THE BALKANS 72

THE BALKAN WARS
1912-1913

BY
Jacob Gould Schurman

PREFACE

The interest in the Balkan Wars of 1912-1913 has exceeded the expectations of the publishers of this volume. The first edition, which was published five months ago, is already exhausted and a second is now called for. Meanwhile there has broken out and is now in progress a war which is generally regarded as the greatest of all time--a war already involving five of the six Great Powers and three of the smaller nations of Europe as well as Japan and Turkey and likely at any time to embroil other countries in Europe, Asia, and Africa, which are already embraced in the area of military operations.

This War of Many Nations had its origin in Balkan situation. It began on July 28 with the declaration of the Dual Monarchy to the effect that from that moment Austria-Hungary was in a state of war with Servia. And the fundamental reason for this declaration as given in the note or ultimatum to Servia was the charge that the Servian authorities had encouraged the Pan-Serb agitation which seriously menaced the integrity of Austria-Hungary and had already caused the assassination at Serajevo of the Heir to the Throne.

No one could have observed at close range the Balkan Wars of 1912-1913 without perceiving, always in the background and occasionally in the foreground, the colossal rival figures of Russia and Austria-Hungary. Attention was called to the phenomenon at various points in this volume and especially in the concluding pages.

The issue of the Balkan struggles of 1912-1913 was undoubtedly favorable to Russia. By her constant diplomatic support she retained the friendship and earned the gratitude of Greece, Montenegro, and Servia; and through her championship, belated though it was, of the claims of Roumania to territorial compensation for benevolent neutrality during the war of the Allies against Turkey, she won the friendship of the predominant Balkan power which had hitherto been regarded as the immovable eastern outpost of the Triple Alliance. But while Russia was victorious she did not gain all that she had planned and hoped for. Her very triumph at Bukarest was a proof that she had lost her influence over Bulgaria. This Slav state after the war against Turkey came under the influence of Austria-Hungary, by whom she was undoubtedly incited to strife with Servia and her other partners in the late war against Turkey. Russia was unable to prevent the second Balkan war between the Allies. The Czar's summons to the Kings of Bulgaria and Servia on June 9, 1913, to submit, in the name of Pan-Slavism, their disputes to his decision failed to produce the desired effect, while this assumption of Russian hegemony in Balkan affairs greatly exacerbated Austro-Hungarian sentiment. That action of the Czar, however, was clear notification and proof to all the world that Russia regarded the Slav States in the Balkans as objects of her peculiar concern and protection.

The first Balkan War--the war of the Allies against Turkey--ended in a way that surprised all the world. Everybody expected a victory for the Turks. That the Turks should one day be driven out of Europe was the universal assumption, but it was the equally fixed belief that the agents of their expulsion would be the Great Powers or some of the Great Powers. That the little independent States of the Balkans should themselves be equal to the task no one imagined,--no one with the possible exception of the government of Russia. And as Russia rejoiced over the victory of the Balkan States and the defeat of her secular Mohammedan neighbor, Austria-Hungary looked on not only with amazement but with disappointment and chagrin.

For the contemporaneous diplomacy of the Austro-Hungarian government was based on the assumption that the Balkan States would be vanquished by Turkey. And its standing policy had been on the one hand to keep the Kingdom of Servia small and weak (for the Dual Monarchy was itself an important Serb state) and on the other hand to broaden her Adriatic possessions and also to make her way through Novi Bazar and Macedonia to Saloniki and the Aegean, when the time came to secure this concession from the Sultan without provoking a European war. It seemed in 1908 as though the favorable moment had arrived to make a first move, and the Austro-Hungarian government put forward a project for connecting the Bosnian and Macedonian railway systems. But the only result was to bring to an end the co-operation which had for some years been maintained between the Austrian and Russian governments in the enforcement upon the Porte of the adoption of reforms in Macedonia.

And now the result of the Balkan Wars of 1912-1913 was the practical expulsion of Turkey from Europe and the territorial aggrandizement of Servia and the sister state of Montenegro through the annexation of those very Turkish domains which lay between the Austro-Hungarian frontier and the Aegean. At every point Austro-Hungarian policies had met with reverses.

Only one success could possibly be attributed to the diplomacy of the Ballplatz. The exclusion of Servia from the Adriatic Sea and the establishment of the independent State of Albania was the achievement of Count Berchtold, the Austro-Hungarian Minister of Foreign Affairs. The new State has been a powder magazine from the beginning, and since the withdrawal of Prince William of Wied, the government, always powerless, has fallen into chaos. Intervention on the part of neighboring states is inevitable. And only last month the southern part of Albania--that is, Northern Epirus--was occupied by a Greek army for the purpose of ending the sanguinary anarchy which has hitherto prevailed. This action will be no surprise to the readers of this volume. The occupation, or rather re-occupation, is declared by the Greek Government to be provisional and it is apparently approved by all the Great Powers. Throughout the rest of Albania similar intervention will be necessary to establish order, and to protect the life and property of the inhabitants without distinction of race, tribe, or creed. Servia might perhaps have governed the country, had she not been compelled by the Great Powers, at the instigation of Austria-Hungary, to withdraw her forces. And her extrusion from the Adriatic threw her back toward the Aegean, with the result of shutting Bulgaria out of Central Macedonia, which was annexed by Greece and Servia presumably under arrangements satisfactory to the latter for an outlet to the sea at Saloniki. The war declared by Austria-Hungary against Servia may be regarded to some extent as an effort to nullify in the interests of the former the enormous advantages which accrued directly to Servia and indirectly to Russia from the Balkan Wars of 1912-1913. That Russia should have come to the support of Servia was as easy to foresee as any future political event whatever. And the action of Germany and France once war had broken out between their respective allies followed as a matter of course. If the Austro-German Alliance wins in the War of Many Nations it will doubtless control the eastern Adriatic and open up a way for itself to the Aegean. Indeed, in that event, German trade and German political influence would spread unchallenged across the continents from the North Sea to the Persian Gulf and the Indian Ocean. Turkey is a friend and ally; but even if Turkey were hostile she would have no strength to resist such victorious powers. And the Balkan States, with the defeat of Russia, would be compelled to recognize Germanic supremacy.

If on the other hand the Allies come out victorious in the War of Many Nations, Servia and perhaps Roumania would be permitted to annex the provinces occupied by their brethren in the Dual Monarchy and Servian expansion to the Adriatic would be assured. The Balkan States would almost inevitably fall under the controlling influence of Russia, who would become mistress of Constantinople and gain an unrestricted outlet to the Mediterranean through the Bosphorus, the Sea of Marmora, and the Dardanelles.

In spite of themselves the destiny of the peoples of the Balkans is once more set on the issue of war. It is not inconceivable, therefore, that some or all of those States may be drawn into the present colossal conflict. In 1912-1913 the first war showed Bulgaria, Greece, Montenegro, and Servia allied against Turkey; and in the second war Greece, Montenegro, and Servia were joined by Roumania in the war against Bulgaria, who was also independently attacked by Turkey. What may happen in 1914 or 1915 no one can predict. But if this terrible conflagration, which is already devastating Europe and convulsing all the continents and vexing all the oceans of the globe, spreads to the Balkans, one may hazard the guess that Greece, Montenegro, Servia, and Roumania will stand together on the side of the Allies and that Bulgaria if she is not carried away by marked Austro-German victories will remain neutral,--unless indeed the other Balkan States win her over, as they not inconceivably might do, if they rose to the heights of unwonted statesmanship by recognizing her claim to that part of Macedonia in which the Bulgarian element predominates but which was ceded to her rivals by the Treaty of Bukarest.

But I have said enough to indicate that as in its origin so also in its results this awful cataclysm under which the civilized world is now reeling will be found to be vitally connected with the Balkan Wars of 1912-1913. And I conclude with the hope that the present volume, which devotes indeed but little space to military matters and none at all to atrocities and massacres, may prove helpful to readers who seek light on the underlying conditions, the causes, and the consequences of those historic struggles. The favor already accorded to the work and the rapid exhaustion of the first edition[1] seem to furnish some justification of this hope.

JACOB GOULD SCHURMAN.
November 26, 1914.

---

1 The present work is rather, a reprint than a new edition, few changes having been made except the correction of typographical errors.

INTRODUCTION

The changes made in the map of Europe by the Balkan Wars of 1912-1913 were not merely the occasion but a cause and probably the most potent, and certainly the most urgent, of all the causes that led to the World War which has been raging with such titanic fury since the summer of 1914.

Had the Balkan Allies after their triumph over Turkey not fallen out amongst themselves, had there been no second Balkan War in 1913, had the Turkish provinces wrested from the Porte by the united arms of Bulgaria, Greece, Servia, and Montenegro been divided amongst the victors either by diplomacy or arbitration substantial justice would have been done to all, none of them would have been humiliated, and their moderation and concord would have commended their achievement to the Great Powers who might perhaps have secured the acquiescence of Austria-Hungary in the necessary enlargement of Servia and the expansion of Greece to Saloniki and beyond.

But the outbreak of the second Balkan War nullified all these fair prospects. And Bulgaria, who brought it on, found herself encircled by enemies, including not only all her recent Allies against Turkey, but also Turkey herself, and even Roumania, who had remained a neutral spectator of the first Balkan War. Of course Bulgaria was defeated. And a terrible punishment was inflicted on her. She was stripped of a large part of the territory she had just conquered from Turkey, including her most glorious battle-fields; her original provinces were dismembered; her extension to the Aegean Sea was seriously obstructed, if not practically blocked; and, bitterest and most tragic of all, the redemption of the Bulgarians in Macedonia, which was the principal object and motive of her war against Turkey in 1912, was frustrated and rendered hopeless by Greek and Servian annexations of Macedonian territory extending from the Mesta to the Drin with the great cities of Saloniki, Kavala, and

Monastir, which in the patriotic national consciousness had long loomed up as fixed points in the "manifest destiny" of Bulgaria.

That the responsibility for precipitating the second Balkan War rests on Bulgaria is demonstrated in the latter portion of this volume. Yet the intransigent and bellicose policy of Bulgaria was from the point of view of her own interests so shortsighted, so perilous, so foolish and insane that it seemed, even at the time, to be directed by some external power and for some ulterior purpose. No proof, however, was then available. But hints of that suspicion were clearly conveyed even in the first edition of this volume, which, it may be recalled, antedates the outbreak of the great European War. Thus, on page 103, the question was put:

"Must we assume that there is some ground for suspecting that Austria-Hungary was inciting Bulgaria to war?"

And again, on page 108, with reference to General Savoff's order directing the attack on the Greek and Servian forces which initiated the second Balkan War, the inquiry was made:

"Did General Savoff act on his own responsibility? Or is there any truth in the charge that King Ferdinand, after a long consultation with the Austro-Hungarian Minister, instructed the General to issue the order?"

These questions may now be answered with positive assurance. What was only surmise when this volume was written is to-day indubitable certainty. The proof is furnished by the highest authorities both Italian and Russian.

When the second Balkan War broke out San Giuliano was Prime Minister of Italy. And he has recently published the fact that at that time--the summer of 1913--the Austro-Hungarian government communicated to the Italian government its intention of making war on Servia and claimed under the terms of the Triple Alliance the co-operation of Italy and Germany. The Italian government repudiated the obligation imputed to it by Austria-Hungary and flatly declared that the Triple Alliance had nothing to do with a war of aggression. That Austria-Hungary did not proceed to declare war against Servia at that time--perhaps because she was discouraged by Germany as well as by Italy--makes it all the more intelligible, in view of her bellicose attitude, that she should have been urgent and insistent in pushing Bulgaria forward to smite their common rival.

This conclusion is confirmed by the positive statement of the Russian government. The communication accompanying the declaration of war against Bulgaria, dated October 18, contains the following passage:

"The victorious war of the united Balkan people against their
ancient enemy, Turkey, assured to Bulgaria an honorable place in
the Slavic family. But under Austro-German suggestion, contrary
to the advice of the Russian Emperor and without the knowledge of
the Bulgarian government, the Coburg Prince on June 29, 1913,
moved Bulgarian armies against the Serbians."

The "Coburg Prince" is of course Ferdinand, King of Bulgaria. That he acted under Austro-Hungarian influences in attacking his Balkan Allies on that fateful Sunday, June 29, 1913, is no longer susceptible of doubt. But whatever other inferences may be drawn from that conclusion it certainly makes the course of Bulgaria in launching the second Balkan War, though its moral character remains unchanged, look less hopeless and desperate than it otherwise appeared. Had she not Austria-Hungary behind her? And had not Austria-Hungary at that very time informed her Italian ally that she intended making war against Servia?

But, whatever the explanation, the thunderbolt forged in 1913 was not launched till July 28, 1914, when Austria-Hungary formally declared war on Servia. The occasion was the assassination, a month earlier, of the heir to the throne, Archduke Franz Ferdinand and his wife, the Duchess of Hohenburg, in the streets of Sarajevo. The occasion, however, was not the cause of the war. The cause was that which moved the Dual Monarchy to announce a war on Servia in the summer of 1913, namely, dissatisfaction with the territorial aggrandizement of Servia as a result of the first Balkan War and alarm at the Pan-Serb agitation and propaganda which followed the Servian victories over Turkey. These motives had subsequently been much intensified by the triumph of Servia over Bulgaria in the second Balkan War.

The relations of Austria-Hungary to Servia had been acutely strained since October, 1908, when the former annexed the Turkish provinces of Bosnia and Herzegovina, which under the terms of the treaty of Berlin she had been administering since 1878. The inhabitants of Bosnia and Herzegovina are Serb, and Serb also are the inhabitants of Dalmatia on the west and Croatia on the north, which the Dual Monarchy had already brought under its sceptre. The new annexation therefore seemed a fatal and a final blow to the national aspirations of the Serb race and it was bitterly resented by those who had already been gathered together and "redeemed" in the Kingdom of Servia. A second disastrous consequence of the annexation was that it left Servia hopelessly land-locked. The Serb population of Dalmatia and Herzegovina looked out on the Adriatic along a considerable section of its eastern coast, but Servia's long-cherished hope of becoming a maritime state by the annexation of the Serb provinces of Bosnia and Herzegovina was now definitively at an end. She protested, she appealed, she threatened; but with Germany behind the Dual Monarchy and Russia still weak from the effects of the war with Japan, she was quickly compelled to submit to superior force.

During the war of the Balkan Allies against Turkey Servia made one more effort to get to the Adriatic,--this time by way of Albania. She marched her forces over the mountains of that almost impassable country and reached the sea at Durazzo. But she was forced back by the European powers at the demand of Austria-Hungary, as some weeks later on the same compulsion she had to withdraw from the siege of Scutari. Then she turned toward the Aegean, and the second Balkan War gave her a new opportunity. The treaty of Bukarest and the convention with Greece assured her of an outlet to the sea at Saloniki. But this settlement proved scarcely less objectionable to Austria-Hungary than the earlier dream of Servian expansion to the Adriatic by the annexation of the Turkish provinces of Bosnia and Herzegovina.

The fact is that, if we look at the matter dispassionately and in a purely objective spirit, we shall find that there really was a hopeless incompatibility between the ideals, aims, policies, and interests of the Servians and the Serb race and those of the Austrians and Hungarians. Any aggrandizement of the Kingdom of Servia, any enlargement of its territory, any extension to the sea and especially to the Adriatic, any heightening and intensifying of the national consciousness of its people involved some danger to the Dual Monarchy. For besides the Germans who control Austria, and the Hungarians who control Hungary, the Austro-Hungarian Empire embraces many millions of Slavs, and the South Slavs are of the same family and speak practically the same language as the inhabitants of the Kingdom of Servia. And Austria and Hungary can not get to their outlets on the Adriatic--Trieste and Fiume--without passing through territory inhabited by these South Slavs.

If, therefore, Austria and Hungary were not to be left land-locked they must at all hazards prevent the absorption of their South Slav subjects by the Kingdom of Servia. Pan-Serbism at once menaced the integrity of the Austro-Hungarian Empire and jeopardized its position on the Adriatic. Hence the cardinal features in the Balkan policy of Austria-Hungary were a ruthless repression of national aspiration among its South Slav subjects--the inhabitants of Croatia, Dalmatia, Bosnia, and Herzegovina; a watchful and jealous opposition to any increase of the territory or resources of the Kingdom of Servia; and a stern and unalterable determination to prevent Servian expansion to the Adriatic.

The new Servia which emerged from the Balkan Wars of 1912-1913 was an object of anxiety and even of alarm to the statesmen of Vienna and Buda-Pesth. The racial and national aspirations already astir among the South Slavs of the Dual Monarchy were quickened and intensified by the great victories won by their Servian brethren over both Turks and Bulgarians and by the spectacle of the territorial aggrandizement which accrued from those victories to the independent Kingdom of Servia. Might not this Greater Servia prove a magnet to draw the kindred Slavs of Bosnia, Herzegovina, Dalmatia, and Croatia away from their allegiance to an alien empire? The diplomacy of Vienna had indeed succeeded in excluding Servia from the Adriatic but it had neither prevented its territorial aggrandizement nor blocked its access to the Aegean.

Access to the Aegean was not, however, as serious a matter as access to the Adriatic. Yet the expansion of Servia to the south over the Macedonian territory she had wrested from Turkey, as legalized in the Treaty of Bukarest, nullified the Austro-Hungarian dream of expansion through Novi Bazar and Macedonia to the Aegean and the development from Saloniki as a base of a great and profitable commerce with all the Near and Middle East.

Here were the conditions of a national tragedy. They have developed into a great international war, the greatest and most terrible ever waged on this planet.

It may be worth while in concluding to note the relations of the Balkan belligerents of 1912-1913 to the two groups of belligerents in the present world-conflict.

The nemesis of the treaties of London and Bukarest and the fear of the Great Powers pursue the Balkan nations and determine their alignments. The declaration of war by Austria-Hungary against Servia, which started the present cataclysm, fixed the enemy status of Servia and also Montenegro. The good relations long subsisting between Emperor William and the Porte were a guarantee to the Central Powers of the support of Turkey, which quickly declared in their favor. The desire of avenging the injury done her by the treaty of Bukarest and the prospect of territorial aggrandizement at the expense of her sister Slav nation on the west drew Bulgaria (which was influenced also by the victories of the Germanic forces) into the same group in company with Turkey, her enemy in both the Balkan Wars of 1912-1913. Bulgaria's opportunity for revenge soon arrived. It was the Bulgarian army, in cooperation with the Austro-German forces, that overran Servia and Montenegro and drove the national armies beyond their own boundaries into foreign territory. If the fortunes of war turn and the Entente Powers get the upper hand in the Balkans, these expelled armies of Servia and Montenegro, who after rest and reorganization and re-equipping in Corfu have this summer been transported by France and England to Saloniki, may have the satisfaction of devastating the territory of the sister Slav state of Bulgaria, quite in the divisive and internecine spirit of all Balkan history. The fate and future of Bulgaria, Servia, and Montenegro now depend on the issue of the great European conflict. The same thing is true of Turkey, into which meanwhile Russian forces, traversing the Caucasus, have driven a dangerous wedge through Armenia towards Mesopotamia. Roumania has thus far maintained the policy of neutrality to which she adhered so successfully in the first Balkan war--a policy which in view of her geographical situation, with Bulgaria to the south, Russia to the north, and Austria-Hungary to the west, she cannot safely abandon till fortune has declared more decisively for one or the other group of belligerents. The only remaining party to the Balkan Wars is Greece, and the situation of Greece, though not tragic like that of Servia, must be exceedingly humiliating to the Greek nation and to the whole Hellenic race.

When the war broke out, Mr. Venizelos was still prime minister of Greece. His policy was to go loyally to the assistance of Servia, as required by the treaty between the two countries; to defend New Greece against Bulgaria, to whom, however, he was ready to make some concessions on the basis of a quid pro quo; and to join and co-operate actively with the Entente Powers on the assurance of receiving territorial compensation in Asia Minor. King Constantine, on the other hand, seems to have held that the war of the Great Powers in the Balkans practically abrogated the treaty between Greece and Servia and that, in any event, Greek resistance to the Central Powers was useless. The positive programme of the King was to maintain neutrality between the two groups of belligerents and at the same time to keep the Greek army mobilized. Between these two policies the Greek nation wavered and hesitated; but the King, who enjoyed the complete confidence of the general staff, had his way and the cabinet of Mr. Venizelos was replaced by another in sympathy with the policy of the neutrality of Greece and the mobilization of the Greek army.

It was, under all the circumstances of the case, an exceedingly difficult policy to carry out successfully. Each group of the belligerents wanted special favors; the nation was divided on the subject of neutrality; the expense of keeping the army mobilized was ruinous to the country; and the views and sympathies of the greatest statesman Modern Greece had ever had remained out of office, as they had been in office, diametrically opposed to those of the victorious warrior-King and doubtless also of the Queen, the sister of the German Emperor. This condition was one of unstable equilibrium which could not long continue. It was upset on May 26, 1916, by a Bulgarian invasion of Greek territory and the seizure of Fort Rupel, one of the keys to the Struma Valley and to eastern Macedonia. The cities of Seres and Drama with their large Greek Population, and even Kavala are now in danger, and the Greek people seem greatly stirred by the situation. Mr. Venizelos in a newspaper article bitterly asks:

> "Who could have imagined a Greek army witnessing the Bulgarian flag replacing that of Greece? Is it for this that our mobilization is maintained?"

But, while Greece has been invaded by Bulgaria, with the support of Germany (who, however, has given a written promise that the Greek territory now occupied shall be restored), Greek sovereignty has since suffered another severe shock by the intervention of Great Britain, France, and Russia, who, under the Protocol of London, are the Protecting Powers of the Kingdom. These Powers demand of the Greek government that the army shall be completely and immediately demobilized, that the present cabinet shall be replaced by another which shall guarantee benevolent neutrality toward the Entente Powers, that the Chamber shall be immediately dissolved and new elections held, and that certain public functionaries obnoxious to the legations of the Allies shall be replaced. And statements from Athens dated June 21 announce that Greece, under the menace of an embargo maintained by the allied navies, has yielded to these demands. With Greece humiliated by the Protecting Powers and her territory occupied by Bulgaria, with Servia and Montenegro overrun and occupied by the German-Austrian-Bulgarian forces, with Roumania waiting to see which of the belligerent groups will be finally victorious, with Bulgaria now basking in the sunshine of the Central Powers but an object of hatred to all the Allied Powers and especially to Russia, one may be pardoned for refusing to make any guess whatever as to the way in which the resultant diagonal of the parallelogram of European forces will ultimately run through the Balkans. Fortunately also such prediction has no place in an account of the Balkan Wars of 1912-1913.

To-day the Balkan nations are the pawns of the Great Powers who are directly responsible for the deplorable conditions that now exist among them. Yet in a very real sense their present tragic situation is the nemesis of the political sins of the Balkan nations themselves. These sins are those of all undeveloped political communities. Even the most highly civilized nations may temporarily fall under their sway, and then civilization reverts to barbarism, as the terrible condition of Europe to-day actually demonstrates. But the acute disease from which Europe suffers is more or less chronic in the Balkans, where elemental human nature has never been thoroughly disciplined and chastened in the school of peaceful political life and experience. Each for himself without regard to others or even without thought of a future day of reckoning seems to be the maxim of national conduct among the Balkan peoples. The spirit of strife and division possesses them; they are dominated by the uncontrolled instinct of national egoism and greed. The second Balkan War, alike in its origin, course, and conclusion, was a bald exhibition of the play of these primitive and hateful passions.

The history of the world, which is also the high tribunal of the world, proves that no nation can with impunity ignore the rights of other nations or repudiate the ideal of a common good or defy the rule of righteousness by which political communities achieve it--justice, moderation, and the spirit of hopeful and unwearying conciliation. In their war against Turkey in 1912 the Balkan nations, for the first time in history, laid aside their mutual antagonisms and co-operated in a common cause. This union and concord marked at least the beginning of political wisdom. And it was vindicated, if ever any policy was vindicated, by the surprise and splendor of the results.

My hope for the Balkan nations is that they may return to this path from which they were too easily diverted in 1913. They must learn, while asserting each its own interests and advancing each its own welfare, to pay scrupulous regard to the rights and just claims of others and to co-operate wisely for the common good in a spirit of mutual confidence and good will. This high policy, as expedient as it is sound, was to a considerable extent embodied in the leadership of Venizelos and Pashitch and Gueshoff. And where there is a leader with vision the people in the end will follow him. May the final settlement of the European War put no unnecessary obstacle in the way of the normal political development of all the Balkan Nations!

J. G. S.

President's Office Cornell University July 13, 1916

Postscript. I remarked in the foregoing Introduction, that Roumania would not abandon her neutrality till fortune had declared more decisively for one or the other group of belligerents. That was written seven weeks ago. And within the last few days Roumania has joined the Allies and declared war against Austria-Hungary. I also noted that the unstable equilibrium which had been maintained in Greece between the party of King Constantine and the party of Venizelos had already been upset to the disadvantage of the former. Roumania's adhesion to the cause of the Allies is bound to accelerate this movement. It would not be surprising if Greece were any day now to follow the example of Roumania. Had Greece in 1914 stood by Venizelos and joined the Allies the chances are that Roumania would at that time have adopted the same course. But the opposition of King Constantine delayed that consummation, directly in the case of Greece, and indirectly in the case of Roumania. Now that the latter has cast in her lot with the Allies and the former is likely at any tune to follow her example, I may be permitted to quote the forecast which I made in the Preface to the Second Edition of this volume under date of November 26, 1914:

"If this terrible conflagration, which is already devastating Europe and convulsing all the continents and vexing all the oceans of the globe, spreads to the Balkans, one may hazard the guess that Greece, Montenegro, Servia, and Roumania will stand together on the side of the Allies and that Bulgaria if she is not carried away by marked Austro-German victories will remain neutral."

J. G. S.
September 1, 1916.

I
TURKEY AND THE BALKAN STATES

The expulsion of the Turks from Europe was long ago written in the book of fate. There was nothing uncertain about it except the date and the agency of destiny.

THE TURKISH EMPIRE IN EUROPE

A little clan of oriental shepherds, the Turks had in two generations gained possession of the whole of the northwest corner of Asia Minor and established themselves on the eastern shore of the Bosphorus. The great city of Brusa, whose groves to-day enshrine the stately beauty of their mosques and sultans' tombs, capitulated to Orkhan, the son of the first Sultan, in 1326; and Nicaea, the cradle of the Greek church and temporary capital of the Greek Empire, surrendered in 1330. On the other side of the Bosphorus Orkhan could see the domes and palaces of Constantinople which, however, for another century was to remain the seat of the Byzantine Empire.

The Turks crossed the Hellespont and, favored by an earthquake, marched in 1358 over the fallen walls and fortifications into the city of Gallipoli. In 1361 Adrianople succumbed to the attacks of Orkhan's son, Murad I, whose sway was soon acknowledged in Thrace and Macedonia, and who was destined to lead the victorious Ottoman armies as far north as the Danube.

But though the provinces of the corrupt and effete Byzantine Empire were falling into the hands of the Turks, the Slavs were still unsubdued. Lazar the Serb threw down the gauntlet to Murad. On the memorable field of Kossovo, in 1389, the opposing forces met--Murad supported by his Asiatic and European vassals and allies, and Lazar with his formidable army of Serbs, Bosnians, Albanians, Poles, Magyars, and Vlachs. Few battles in the world have produced such a deep and lasting impression as this battle of Kossovo, in which the Christian nations after long and stubborn resistance were vanquished by the Moslems. The Servians still sing ballads which cast a halo of pathetic romance round their great disaster. And after more than five centuries the Montenegrins continue to wear black on their caps in mourning for that fatal day.

In the next two centuries the Ottoman Empire moved on toward the zenith of its glory. Mohammed II conquered Constantinople in 1453. And in 1529 Suleyman the Magnificent was at the gates of Vienna. Suleyman's reign forms the climax of Turkish history. The Turks had become a central European power occupying Hungary and menacing Austria. Suleyman's dominions extended from Mecca to Buda-Pesth and from Bagdad to Algiers. He commanded the Mediterranean, the Euxine, and the Red Sea, and his navies threatened the coasts of India and Spain.

But the conquests of the Turks were purely military. They did nothing for their subjects, whom they treated with contempt, and they wanted nothing from them but tribute and plunder. As the Turks were always numerically inferior to the aggregate number of the peoples under their sway, their one standing policy was to keep them divided--divide et impera. To fan racial and religious differences among their subjects was to perpetuate the rule of the masters. The whole task of government, as the Turks conceived it, was to collect tribute from the conquered and keep them in subjection by playing off their differences against one another.

But a deterioration of Turkish rulers set in soon after the time of Suleyman with a corresponding decline in the character and efficiency of the army. And the growth of Russia and the reassertion of Hungary, Poland, and Austria were fatal to the maintenance of an alien and detested empire founded on military domination alone. By the end of the seventeenth century the Turks had been driven out of Austria, Hungary, Transylvania, and Podolia, and the northern boundaries of their Empire were fixed by the Carpathians, the Danube, and the Save. How marked and rapid was the further decline of the Ottoman Empire may be inferred from the fact that twice in the eighteenth century Austria and Russia discussed the project of dividing it between them. But the inevitable disintegration of the Turkish dominion was not to inure to the glorification of any of the Great Powers, though Russia certainly contributed to the weakening of the common enemy. The decline and diminution of the Ottoman Empire continued throughout the nineteenth century. What happened, however, was the revolt of subject provinces and the creation out of the territory of European Turkey of the independent states of Greece, Servia, Roumania, and Bulgaria. And it was Bulgarians, Greeks, and Servians, with the active assistance of the Montenegrins and the benevolent neutrality of the Roumanians, who, in the war of 1912-1913, drove the Turk out of Europe, leaving him nothing but the city of Constantinople and a territorial fringe bordered by the Chataldja line of fortifications.

THE EARLIER SLAV EMPIRES

There is historic justice in the circumstance that the Turkish Empire in Europe met its doom at the hands of the Balkan nations themselves. For these nationalities had been completely submerged and even their national consciousness annihilated under centuries of Moslem intolerance, misgovernment, oppression, and cruelty.

None suffered worse than Bulgaria, which lay nearest to the capital of the Mohammedan conqueror. Yet Bulgaria had had a glorious, if checkered, history long before there existed any Ottoman Empire either in Europe or in Asia. From the day their sovereign Boris accepted Christianity in 864 the Bulgarians had made rapid and conspicuous progress in their ceaseless conflicts with the Byzantine Empire. The Bulgarian church was recognized as independent by the Greek patriarch at Constantinople; its primates subsequently received the title of patriarch, and their see was established at Preslav, and then successively westward at Sofia, Vodena, Presba, and finally Ochrida, which looks out on the mountains of Albania. Under Czar Simeon, the son of Boris, "Bulgaria," says Gibbon, "assumed a rank among the civilized powers of the earth." His dominions extended from the Black Sea to the Adriatic and comprised the greater part of Macedonia, Greece, Albania, Servia, and Dalmatia; leaving only to the Byzantine Empire--whose civilization he introduced and sedulously promoted among the Bulgarians--the cities of Constantinople, Saloniki, and Adrianople with the territory immediately surrounding them. But this first Bulgarian Empire was shortlived, though the western part remained independent under Samuel, who reigned, with Ochrida as his capital, from 976 to 1014. Four years later the Byzantine Emperor, Basil II, annihilated the power of Samuel, and for a hundred and fifty years the Bulgarian people remained subject to the rule of Constantinople. In 1186 under the leadership of the brothers Asen they regained their independence. And the reign of Czar Asen II (1218-1240) was the most prosperous period of all Bulgarian history. He restored the Empire of Simeon, his boast being that he had left to the Byzantines nothing but Constantinople and the cities round it, and he encouraged commerce, cultivated arts and letters, founded and endowed churches and monasteries, and embellished his capital, Trnovo, with beautiful and magnificent buildings. After Asen came a period of decline culminating in a humiliating defeat by the Servians in 1330. The quarrels of the Christian races of the Balkans facilitated the advance of the Moslem invader, who overwhelmed the Serbs and their allies on the memorable field of Kossovo in 1389, and four years later captured and burned the Bulgarian capital, Trnovo, Czar Shishman himself perishing obscurely in the common destruction. For five centuries Bulgaria remained under Moslem despotism, we ourselves being the witnesses of her emancipation in the last thirty-five years.

The fate of the Serbs differed only in degree from that of the Bulgarians. Converted to Christianity in the middle of the ninth century, the major portion of the race remained till the twelfth century under either Bulgarian or Byzantine sovereignty. But Stephen Nemanyo bought under his rule Herzegovina, Montenegro and part of modern Servia and old Servia, and on his abdication in 1195 in favor of his son launched a royal dynasty which reigned over the Serb people for two centuries. Of that line the most distinguished member was Stephen Dushan, who reigned from 1331 to 1355. He wrested the whole of the Balkan Peninsula from the Byzantine Emperor, and took Belgrade, Bosnia, and Herzegovina from the King of Hungary. He encouraged literature, gave to his country a highly advanced code of laws, and protected the church whose head--the Archbishop of Ipek--he raised to the dignity of patriarch. On Easter Day 1346 he had himself crowned at Uskub as "Emperor of the Greeks and Serbs." A few years later he embarked on an enterprise by which, had he been successful, he might have changed the course of European history. It was nothing less than the capture of Constantinople and the union of Serbs, Bulgarians, and Greeks into an empire which might defend Christendom against the rising power of Islam. Dushan was within forty miles of his goal with an army of 80,000 men when he died suddenly in camp on the 20th of December, 1355. Thirty-four years later Dushan's countrymen were annihilated by the Turks at Kossovo! All the Slavonic peoples of the Balkan Peninsula save the brave mountaineers of Montenegro came under Moslem subjection. And under Moslem subjection they remained till the nineteenth century.

TURKISH OPPRESSION OF SLAVS

It is impossible to give any adequate description of the horrors of Turkish rule in these Christian countries of the Balkans. Their people, disqualified from holding even the smallest office, were absolutely helpless under the oppression of their foreign masters, who ground them down under an intolerable load of taxation and plunder. The culminating cruelty was the tribute of Christian children from ten to twelve years of age who were sent to Constantinople to recruit the corps of janissaries. It is not surprising that for the protection of wives and children and the safeguarding of interests the nobles of Bosnia and the Pomaks of Southeastern Bulgaria embraced the creed of their conquerors; the wonder is that the people as a whole remained true to their Christian faith even at the cost of daily martyrdom from generation to generation. Their fate too grew worse as the Turkish power declined after the unsuccessful siege of Vienna in 1683. For at first Ottoman troops ravaged Bulgaria as they marched through the land on their way to Austria; and later disbanded soldiers in defiance of Turkish authority plundered the country and committed nameless atrocities. Servia was to some extent protected by her remote location, but that very circumstance bred insubordination in the janissaries, who refused to obey the local Turkish governors and gave themselves up to looting, brigandage, and massacre. The national spirt of the subject races was completely crushed. The Servians and Bulgarians for three or four centuries lost all consciousness of a fatherland. The countrymen of Simeon and Dushan became mere hewers of wood and drawers of water for their foreign masters. Servia and Bulgaria simply disappeared. As late as 1834 Kinglake in travelling to Constantinople from Belgrade must have passed straight across Bulgaria. Yet in "Eothen," in which he describes his travels, he never even mentions that country or its people.

It is easy to understand that this history of Turkish horrors should have burned itself into the heart and soul of the resurrected Servia and Bulgaria of our own day. But there is another circumstance connected with the ruthless destruction and long entombment of these nationalities which it is difficult for foreigners, even the most intelligent foreigners, to understand or at any rate to grasp in its full significance. Yet the sentiments to which that circumstance has given rise and which it still nourishes are as potent a factor in contemporary Balkan politics as the antipathy of the Christian nations to their former Moslem oppressors.

GREEK ECCLESIASTICAL DOMINATION OF SLAV

I refer to the special and exceptional position held by the Greeks in the Turkish dominions. Though the Moslems had possessed themselves of the Greek Empire from the Bosphorus to the Danube, Greek domination still survived as an intellectual, ecclesiastical, and commercial force. The nature and effects of that supremacy, and its results upon the fortunes of other Balkan nations, we must now proceed to consider.

The Turkish government classifies its subjects not on the basis of nationality but on the basis of religion. A homogeneous religious group is designated a millet or nation. Thus the Moslems form the millet of Islam. And at the present time there are among others a Greek millet, a Catholic millet, and a Jewish millet. But from the first days of the Ottoman conquest until very recent times all the Christian population, irrespective of denominational differences, was assigned by the Sultans to the Greek millet, of which the patriarch of Constantinople was the head. The members of this millet were all called Greeks; the bishops and higher clergy were exclusively Greek; and the language of their churches and schools was Greek, which was also the language of literature, commerce, and polite society. But the jurisdiction of the patriarch was not restricted even to ecclesiastical and educational matters. It extended to a considerable part of civil law--notably to questions of marriage, divorce, and inheritance when they concerned Christians only.

It is obvious that the possession by the Greek patriarch of Constantinople of this enormous power over the Christian subjects of the Turks enabled him to carry on a propaganda of hellenization. The disappearance for three centuries of the national consciousness in Servia and Bulgaria was not the sole work of the Moslem invader; a more fatal blight to the national languages and culture were the Greek bishops and clergy who conducted their churches and schools. And if Kinglake knew nothing of Bulgaria as late as 1834 it was because every educated person in that country called himself a Greek. For it cannot be too strongly emphasized that until comparatively recent times all Christians of whatever nation or sect were officially recognized by the Turks as members of the Greek millet and were therefore designated Greeks.

The hostility of the Slavonic peoples in the Balkans, and especially of the Bulgarians, to the Greeks, grows out of the ecclesiastical and educational domination which the Greek clergy and bishops so long and so relentlessly exercised over them. Of course the Turkish Sultans are responsible for the arrangement. But there is no evidence that they had any other intention than to rid themselves of a disagreeable task. For the rest they regarded Greeks and Slavs with equal contempt. But the Greeks quickly recognized the racial advantage of their ecclesiastical hegemony. And it was not in human nature to give it up without a struggle. The patriarchate retained its exclusive jurisdiction over all orthodox populations till 1870, when the Sultan issued a firman establishing the Bulgarian exarchate.

There were two other spheres in which Greek influence was paramount in the Turkish Empire. The Turk is a soldier and farmer; the Greek is pre-eminent as a trader, and his ability secured him a disproportionate share of the trade of the empire. Again, the Greeks of Constantinople and other large cities gradually won the confidence of the Turks and attained political importance. During the eighteenth century the highest officials in the empire were invariably Phanariots, as the Constantinople Greeks were termed from the quarter of the city in which they resided.

In speaking of the Greeks I have not had in mind the inhabitants of the present kingdom of Greece. Their subjection by the Turks was as complete as that of the Serbs and Bulgaria though of course they were exempt from ecclesiastical domination at the hands of an alien clergy speaking a foreign language. The enmity of the Bulgarians may to-day be visited upon the subjects of King Constantine, but it was not their ancestors who imposed upon Bulgaria foreign schools and churches but the Greeks of Constantinople and Thrace, over whom the government of Athens has never had jurisdiction.

SERVIAN INDEPENDENCE

So much of the Balkan countries under Turkish rule. Their emancipation did not come till the nineteenth century. The first to throw off the yoke was Servia. Taking advantage of the disorganization and anarchy prevailing in the Ottoman Empire the Servian people rose in a body against their oppressors in January, 1804. Under the able leadership first of Kara-George and afterward of Milosh Obrenovich, Servian autonomy was definitely established in 1817. The complete independence of the country was recognized by the Treaty of Berlin in 1878. The boundaries of the new state, however, fell far short of Servian aspirations, excluding as they did large numbers of the Servian population. The first ruling prince of modern Servia was Milosh Obrenovich; and the subsequent rulers have belonged either to the Obrenovich dynasty or to its rival the dynasty of Kara-George. King Peter, who came to the throne in 1903, is a member of the latter family.

GREEK INDEPENDENCE

Scarcely had Servia won her freedom when the Greek war of independence broke out. Archbishop Germanos called the Christian population of the Morea under the standard of the cross in 1821. For three years the Greeks, with the assistance of European money and volunteers (of whom Lord Byron was the most illustrious), conducted a successful campaign against the Turkish forces; but after the Sultan had in 1824 summoned to his aid Mehemet Ali, Pasha of Egypt, with his powerful fleet and disciplined army, the laurels which the Greek patriots had won were recovered by the oppressor; and, with the recapture of Athens in May, 1827, the whole country once more lay under the dominion of the Turks. The Powers now recognized that nothing but intervention could save Greece for European civilization. The Egyptian fleet was annihilated at Navarino in October, 1828, by the fleets of England, France, and Russia. Greece was constituted an independent monarchy, though the Powers who recognized its independence traced the frontier of the emancipated country in a jealous and niggardly spirit. Prince Otto of Bavaria was designated the first King and reigned for thirty years. He was succeeded in 1863 by King George who lived to see the northern boundary of his kingdom advanced to Saloniki, where, like a faithful sentinel at his post, he fell, on March 18, 1913, by the hand of an assassin just as he had attained the glorious fruition of a reign of fifty years.

BULGARIAN INDEPENDENCE

There had been a literary revival preceding the dawn of independence in Greece. In Bulgaria, which was the last of the Balkan states to become independent, the national regeneration was also fostered by a literary and educational movement, of which the founding of the first Bulgarian school--that of Gabrovo--in 1835 was undoubtedly the most important event. In the next five years more than fifty Bulgarian schools were established and five Bulgarian printing-presses set up. The Bulgarians were beginning to re-discover their own nationality. Bulgarian schools and books produced a reaction against Greek culture and the Greek clergy who maintained it. Not much longer would Greek remain the language of the upper classes in Bulgarian cities; not much longer would ignorant peasants, who spoke only Bulgarian, call themselves Greek. The days of the spiritual domination of the Greek patriarchate were numbered. The ecclesiastical ascendency of the Greeks had crushed Bulgarian nationality more completely than even the civil power of the Turks. The abolition of the spiritual rule of foreigners and the restoration of the independent Bulgarian church became the leading object of the literary reformers, educators, and patriots. It was a long and arduous campaign--a campaign of education and awakening at home and of appeal and discussion in Constantinople. Finally the Sultan intervened and in 1870 issued a firman establishing the Bulgarian exarchate, conferring on it immediate jurisdiction over fifteen dioceses, and providing for the addition of other dioceses on a vote of two-thirds of their Christian population. The new Bulgarian exarch was immediately excommunicated by the

Greek patriarch. But the first and most important official step had been taken in the development of Bulgarian nationality.

The revolt against the Turks followed in 1876. It was suppressed by acts of cruelty and horror unparalleled even in the Balkans. Many thousands of men, women, and children were massacred and scores of villages destroyed. I remember vividly--for I was then in England--how Gladstone's denunciation of those atrocities aroused a wave of moral indignation and wrath which swept furiously from one end of Great Britain to the other, and even aroused the governments and peoples of the Continent of Europe. The Porte refusing to adopt satisfactory measures of reform, Russia declared war and her victorious army advanced to the very gates of Constantinople. The Treaty of San Stefano, which Russia then enforced upon Turkey, created a "Big Bulgaria" that extended from the Black Sea to the Albanian Mountains and from the Danube to the Aegean, leaving to Turkey, however, Adrianople, Saloniki, and the Chalcidician Peninsula. But this treaty was torn to pieces by the Powers, who feared that "Big Bulgaria" would become a mere Russian dependency, and they substituted for it the Treaty of Berlin. Under this memorable instrument, which dashed to the ground the racial and national aspirations of the Bulgarians which the Treaty of San Stefano had so completely satisfied, their country was restricted to a "tributary principality" lying between the Danube and the Balkans, Eastern Roumelia to the south being excluded from it and made an autonomous province of Turkey. This breach in the political life of the race was healed in 1885 by the union of Eastern Roumelia with Bulgaria; and the Ottoman sovereignty, which had become little more than a form, was completely ended in 1908 when the ruler of the enlarged principality of Bulgaria publicly proclaimed it an independent kingdom. In spite of a protest from the Porte the independence of Bulgaria was at once recognized by the Powers.

If Bulgaria owed the freedom with which the Treaty of Berlin dowered her to the swords, and also to the pens, of foreigners, her complete independence was her own achievement. But it was not brought about till a generation after the Treaty of Berlin had recognized the independence of Servia, Montenegro, and Roumania and delegated to Austria-Hungary the administration of Bosnia and Herzegovina. Yet the progress made by Bulgaria first under Prince Alexander and especially since 1887 under Prince Ferdinand (who subsequently assumed the title of King and later of Czar) is one of the most astonishing phenomena in the history of Modern Europe.

THE BALKAN COUNTRIES

Thus in consequence of the events we have here so hastily sketched Turkey had lost since the nineteenth century opened a large portion of the Balkan Peninsula. Along the Danube and the Save at the north Bulgaria and Servia had become independent kingdoms and Bosnia and Herzegovina had at first practically and later formally been annexed to Austria-Hungary. At the extreme southern end of the Balkan Peninsula the Greeks had carved out an independent kingdom extending from Cape Matapan to the Vale of Tempe and the Gulf of Arta. All that remained of European Turkey was the territory lying between Greece and the Slav countries of Montenegro, Bosnia, Servia, and Bulgaria. The Porte has divided this domain into six provinces or vilayets, besides Constantinople and its environs. These vilayets are Scutari and Janina on the Adriatic; Kossovo and Monastir, adjoining them on the east; next Saloniki, embracing the centre of the area; and finally Adrianople, extending from the Mesta River to the Black Sea. In ordinary language the ancient classical names are generally used to designate these divisions. The vilayet of Adrianople roughly corresponds to Thrace, the Adriatic vilayets to Epirus, and the intervening territory to Macedonia. Parts of the domain in question are, however, also known under other names. The district immediately south of Servia is often called Old Servia; and the Adriatic coast lands between Montenegro and Greece are generally designated Albania on the north and Epirus on the south.

The area of Turkey in Europe in 1912 was 169,300 square kilometers; of Bulgaria 96,300; of Greece 64,600; of Servia 48,300; and of Montenegro 9,000. The population of European Turkey at the same date was 6,130,000; of Bulgaria 4,329,000; of Greece 2,632,000; of Servia 2,912,000; and of Montenegro 250,000. To the north of the Balkan states, with the Danube on the south and the Black Sea on the east, lay Roumania having an area of 131,350 square kilometers and a population of 7,070,000.

CAUSES OF THE FIRST BALKAN WAR

What was the occasion of the war between Turkey and the Balkan states in 1912? The most general answer that can be given to that question is contained in the one word Macedonia. Geographically Macedonia lies between Greece, Servia, and Bulgaria. Ethnographically it is an extension of their races. And if, as Matthew Arnold declared, the primary impulse both of individuals and of nations is the tendency to expansion, Macedonia both in virtue of its location and of its population was foreordained to be a magnet to the emancipted Christian nations of the Balkans. Of course the expansion of Greeks and Slavs meant the expulsion of Turks. Hence the Macedonian question was the quintessence of the Near Eastern Question.

But apart altogether from the expansionist ambitions and the racial sympathies of their kindred in Bulgaria, Servia, and Greece, the population of Macedonia had the same right to emancipation from Turkish domination and oppression as their brethren in these neighboring states. The Moslems had forfeited their sovereign rights in Europe by their unutterable incapacity to govern their Christian subjects. Had the Treaty of Berlin sanctioned, instead of undoing, the Treaty of San Stefano, the whole of Macedonia would have come under Bulgarian sovereignty; and although Servia and especially Greece would have protested against the Bulgarian absorption of their Macedonian brethren (whom they had always hoped to bring under their own jurisdiction when the Turk was expelled) the result would certainly have been better for all the Christian inhabitants of Macedonia as well as for the Mohammedans (who number 800,000 persons or nearly one third of the entire population of Macedonia). As it was these, people were all doomed to a continuation of Turkish misgovernment, oppression, and slaughter. The Treaty of Berlin indeed provided for reforms, but the Porte through diplomacy and delay frustrated all the efforts of Europe to have them put into effect. For fifteen years the people waited for the fulfilment of the European promise of an amelioration of their condition, enduring meanwhile the scandalous misgovernment of Abdul Hamid II. But after 1893 revolutionary societies became active. The Internal Organization was a local body whose programme was "Macedonia for the Macedonians." But both in Bulgaria and in Greece there were organized societies which sent insurgent bands into Macedonia to maintain and assert their respective national interests. This was one of the causes of the war between Turkey and Greece in 1897, and the reverses of the Greeks in that war inured to the advantage of the Bulgarian propaganda in Macedonia. Servian bands soon after began to appear on the scene. These hostile activities in Macedonia naturally produced reprisals at the hands of the Turkish authorities. In one district alone 100 villages were burned, over 8,000 houses destroyed, and 60,000 peasants left without homes at the beginning of winter. Meanwhile the Austrian and Russian governments intervened and drew up elaborate schemes of reform, but their plans could not be adequately enforced and the result was failure. The Austro-Russian entente came to an end in 1908, and in the same year England joined Russia in a project aiming at a better administration of justice and involving more effective European supervision. Scarcely had this programme been announced when the revolution under the Young Turk party broke out which promised to the world a regeneration of the Ottoman Empire. Hopeful of these constitutional reformers of Turkey, Europe withdrew from Macedonia and entrusted its destinies to its new master. Never was there a more bitter disappointment. If autocratic Sultans had punished the poor Macedonians with whips, the Young Turks flayed them with scorpions.

Sympathy, indignation, and horror conspired with nationalistic aspirations and territorial interests to arouse the kindred populations of the surrounding states. And in October, 1912, war was declared against Turkey by Bulgaria, Servia, Montenegro, and Greece.

THE BALKAN LEAGUE

This brings us to the so-called Balkan Alliance about which much has been written and many errors ignorantly propagated. For months after the outbreak of the war against Turkey the development of this Alliance into a Confederation of the Balkan states, on the model of the American or the German constitution, was a theme of constant discussion in Europe and America. As a matter of fact there existed no juridical ground for this expectation, and the sentiments of the peoples of the four Christian nations, even while they fought together against the Moslem, were saturated with such an infusion of suspicion and hostility as to render nugatory any programme of Balkan confederation. An alliance had indeed been concluded between Greece and Bulgaria in May, 1912, but it was a defensive, not an offensive alliance. It provided that in case Turkey attacked either of these states, the other should come to its assistance with all its forces, and that whether the object of the attack were the territorial integrity of the nation or the rights guaranteed it by international law or special conventions. Without the knowledge of the Greek government, an offensive alliance against Turkey had in March, 1912, been concluded between Servia and Bulgaria which determined their respective military obligations in case of war and the partition between them, in the event of victory, of the conquered Turkish provinces in Europe. A similar offensive and defensive alliance between Greece and Turkey was under consideration, but before the plan was matured Bulgaria and Servia had decided to declare war against Turkey. This decision had been hastened by the Turkish massacres at Kochana and Berane, which aroused the deepest indignation, especially in Bulgaria. Servia and Bulgaria informed Greece that in three days they would mobilize their forces for the purpose of imposing reforms on Turkey, and, if within a specified time they did not receive a satisfactory reply, they would invade the Ottoman territory and declare war. They invited Greece on this short notice to co-operate with them by a simultaneous mobilization. It was a critical moment not only for the little kingdom of King George, but for that great cause of Hellenism which for thousands of years had animated, and which still animated, the souls of the Greek population in all Aegean lands.

GREECE AND THE LEAGUE

King George himself was a ruler of large experience, of great practical wisdom, and of fine diplomatic skill. He had shortly before selected as prime minister the former Cretan insurgent, Mr. Eleutherios Venizelos. It is significant that the new premier had also taken the War portfolio. He foresaw the impending conflict--as every wise statesman in Europe had foreseen it--and began to make preparations for it. For the reorganization of the army and navy he secured French and English experts, the former headed by General Eydoux, the latter by Admiral Tufnel. By 1914 it was estimated that the military and naval forces of the country would be thoroughly trained and equipped, and war was not expected before that date. But now in 1912 the hand of the Greek government was forced. And a decision one way or the other was inevitable.

Mr. Venizelos had already proved himself an agitator, an orator, and a politician. He was now to reveal himself not only to Greece but to Europe as a wise statesman and an effective leader of his people. The first test came in his answer to the invitation to join Bulgaria and Servia within three days in a war against Turkey. Of all possibilities open to him Mr. Venizelos rejected the programme of continued isolation for Greece. There were those who glorified it as splendid and majestic: to him under the existing circumstances it seemed stupid in itself and certain to prove disastrous in its results. Greece alone would never have been able to wage a war against Turkey. And if Greece declined to participate in the inevitable conflict, which the action of the two Slav states had only hastened, then whether they won or Turkey won, Greece was bound to lose. It was improbable that the Ottoman power should come out of the contest victorious; but, if the unexpected happened, what would be the position, not only of the millions of Greeks in the Turkish Empire, but of the little kingdom of Greece itself on whose northern boundary the insolent Moslem oppressor, flushed with his triumph over Bulgaria, Servia, and Montenegro, would be immovably entrenched? On the other hand if these Christian states themselves should succeed, as seemed likely, in destroying the Ottoman Empire in Europe, the Kingdom of Greece, if she now remained a passive spectator of their struggles, would find in the end that Macedonia had come into the possession of the victorious Slavs, and the Great Idea of the Greeks--the idea of expansion into Hellenic lands eastward toward Constantinople--exploded as an empty bubble. It was Mr. Venizelos's conclusion that Greece could not avoid participating in the struggle. Neutrality would have entailed the complete bankruptcy of Hellenism in the Orient. There remained only the alternative of co-operation--co-operation with Turkey or co-operation with the Christian states of the Balkans.

GREEK AND BULGARIAN ANTIPATHIES

How near Greece was to an alliance with Turkey the world may never know. At the nothing of the sort was even suspected. It was not until Turkey had been overpowered by the forces of the four Christian states and the attitude of Bulgaria toward the other three on the question of the division of the conquered territories had become irreconcilable and menacing that Mr. Venizelos felt it proper to communicate to the Greek people the history of the negotiations by which the Greek government had bound their country to a partner now felt to be so unreasonable and greedy. Feeling in Greece was running high against Bulgaria. The attacks on Mr. Venizelos's government were numerous and bitter. He was getting little or no credit for the victory that had been won against Turkey, while his opponents denounced him for sacrificing the fruits of that victory to Bulgaria. The Greek nation especially resented the occupation by Bulgarian troops of the Aegean coast lands with their large Hellenic population which lay between the Struma and the Mesta including the cities of Seres and Drama and especially Kavala with its fine harbor and its hinterland famed for crops of choice tobacco.

It was on the fourth of July, 1913, a few days after the outbreak of the war between Bulgaria and her late allies, that Mr. Venizelos made his defence in an eloquent and powerful speech at a special session of the Greek parliament. The accusation against him was not only that during the late war he had sacrificed Greek interests to Bulgaria but that he had committed a fatal blunder in joining her in the campaign against Turkey. His reply was that since Greece could not stand alone he had to seek allies in the Balkans, and that it was not his fault if the choice had fallen on Bulgaria. He had endeavored to maintain peace with Turkey. Listen to his own words:

"I did not seek war against the Ottoman Empire. I would not have sought war at a later date if I could have obtained any adjustment of the Cretan question-- that thorn in the side of Greece which can no longer be left as it is without rendering a normal political life absolutely impossible for us. I endeavored to adjust this question, to continue the policy of a close understanding with the neighboring empire, in the hope of obtaining in this way the introduction of reforms which would render existence tolerable to the millions of Greeks within the Ottoman Empire."

THE CRETAN PROBLEM

It was this Cretan question, even more than the Macedonian question, which in 1897 had driven Greece, single-handed and unprepared, into a war with Turkey in which she was destined to meet speedy and overwhelming defeat. It was this same "accursed Cretan question," as Mr. Venizelos called it, which now drew the country into a military alliance against her Ottoman neighbor who, until too late, refused to make any concession either to the just claims of the Cretans or to the conciliatory proposals of the Greek government.

Lying midway between three continents, the island of Crete has played a large part both in ancient and modern history. The explorations and excavations of Sir Arthur Evans at Cnossus seem to prove that the Homeric civilization of Tiryns and Mycenae was derived from Crete, whose earliest remains carry us back three thousand years before the Christian era. And if Crete gave to ancient Greece her earliest civilization she has insisted on giving herself to modern Greece. It is a natural union; for the Cretans are Greeks, undiluted with Turk, Albanian, or Slav blood, though with some admixture of Italian. The one obstacle to this marriage of kindred souls has been Turkey. For Crete was taken from the Venetians by the Turks in 1669, after a twenty years' siege of Candia, the capital. A portion of the inhabitants embraced the creed of their conquerors, so that at the present time perhaps two-thirds of the population are Christian and one-third Moslem. The result has been to make Crete the worst governed province of the Ottoman Empire. In Turkey in Europe diversity of race has kept the Christians quarreling with one another; in Crete diversity of religion plunges the same race into internecine war as often as once in ten years. The island had been the scene of chronic insurrections all through the nineteenth century. Each ended as a rule with a promise of the Sultan to confer upon the Cretans some form of local self-government, with additional privileges, financial or other. But these promises were never fulfilled. Things went from bad to worse. The military intervention of Greece in 1897 led to war with Turkey in which she was disastrously defeated. The European Powers had meantime intervened and they decided that Crete should be endowed with autonomy under the sovereignty of the Sultan, and in 1898 they appointed Prince George of Greece as High Commissioner. Between the political parties of the island and the representatives of the Powers the Prince, who worked steadily for the welfare of Crete, had a difficult task, and in 1906 he withdrew, his successor being Mr. Zaimis, a former prime minister of Greece. The new commissioner was able to report to the protecting Powers in 1908 that a gendarmerie had been established, that tranquility was being maintained, and that the Moslem population enjoyed safety and security. Thereupon the Powers began to withdraw their forces from the island. And the project for annexation with Greece, which had been proclaimed by the Cretan insurgents under Mr. Venizelos in 1905 and which the insular assembly had hastened to endorse, was once more voted by the assembly, who went on to provide for the government of the island in the name of the King of Greece. I have not time to follow in detail the history of this programme of annexation. Suffice it to say that the Cretans ultimately went so far as to elect members to sit in the Greek Parliament at Athens, and that Turkey had given notice that their admission to the chamber would be regarded as a casus belli. I saw them on their arrival in Athens in October 1912, where they received a most enthusiastic welcome from the Greeks, while everybody stopped to admire their picturesque dress, their superb physique, and their dignified demeanor. If Mr. Venizelos excluded these delegates from the chamber he would defy the sentiments of the Greek people. If he admitted them, Turkey would proclaim war.

MR. VENIZELOS'S SOLUTION

The course actually pursued by Mr. Venizelos in this predicament he himself explained to the parliament in the speech delivered at the close of the war against Turkey from which I have already quoted. He declared to his astonished countrymen that in his desire to reach a close understanding with Turkey he had arrived at the point where he no longer demanded a union of Crete with Greece, "knowing it was too much for the Ottoman Empire." What he did ask for was the recognition of the right of the Cretan deputies to sit in the Greek chamber, while Crete itself should remain an autonomous state under the sovereignty of the Sultan. Nay, Mr. Venizelos was so anxious to prevent war with Turkey that he made another concession, for which, he frankly confessed, his political opponents if things had turned out differently would have impeached him for high treason. He actually proposed, in return for the recognition of the right of the Cretan deputies to sit in the Greek chamber, that Greece should pay on behalf of Crete an annual tribute to the Porte.

Happily for Mr. Venizelos's government the Young Turk party who then governed the Ottoman Empire rejected all these proposals. Meanwhile their misgovernment and massacre of Christians in Macedonia were inflaming the red Slav nations and driving them into War against Turkey. When matters had reached a crisis, the reactionary and incompetent Young Turk party were forced out of power and a wise and prudent statesman, the venerable Kiamil Pasha, succeeded to the office of Grand Vizier. He was all for conciliation and compromise with the Greek government, whom he had often warned against an alliance with Bulgaria, and he had in readiness a solution of the Cretan question which he was certain would be satisfactory to both Greece and Turkey. But these concessions were now too late. Greece had decided to throw in her lot with Servia and Bulgaria. And a decree was issued for the mobilization of the Greek troops.

THE WAR

There is not time, nor have I the qualifications, to describe the military operations which followed. In Greece the Crown Prince was appointed commanding general, and the eve proved him one of the great captains of our day. The prime minister, who was also minister of war, furnished him with troops and munitions and supplies. The plains and hills about Athens were turned into mock battlefields for the training of raw recruits; and young Greeks from all parts of the world-- tens of thousands of them from America--poured in to protect the fatherland and to fight the secular enemy of Europe. The Greek government had undertaken to raise an army of 125,000 men to co-operate with the Allies; it was twice as large a number as even the friends of Greece dreamed possible; yet before the war closed

King Constantine had under his banner an army of 250,000 men admirably armed, clothed, and equipped;--each soldier indeed having munitions fifty per cent in excess of the figure fixed by the general staff.

GREEK MILITARY AND NAVAL OPERATIONS

The Greek army, which had been concentrated at Larissa, entered Macedonia by the Pass and the valley of the Xerias River. The Turks met the advancing force at Elassona but retired after a few hours' fighting. They took their stand at the pass of Sarandaporon, from which they were driven by a day's hard fighting on the part of the Greek army and the masterly tactics of the Crown Prince. On October 23 the Greeks were in possession of Serndje. Thence they pushed forward on both sides of the Aliakmon River toward Veria, which the Crown Prince entered with his staff on the morning of October 30. They had covered 150 miles from Larissa, with no facilities but wagons for feeding the army and supplying ammunition. But at Veria they struck the line of railway from Monastir to Saloniki. Not far away was Jenitsa, where the Turkish army numbering from 35,000 to 40,000 had concentrated to make a stand for the protection of Saloniki. The battle of Jenitsa was fiercely contested but the Greeks were victorious though they lost about 2000 men. This victory opened the way to Saloniki. The Turkish armies which defended it having been scattered by the Greek forces, that city surrendered to Crown Prince Constantine on the eighth of November. It was only three weeks since the Greek army had left Larissa and it had disposed of about 60,000 Turks on the way.

On the outbreak of war Greece had declared a blockade of all Turkish ports. To the usual list of contraband articles there were added not only coal, concerning which the practice of belligerent nations had varied, but also machine oil, which so far as I know was then for the first time declared contraband of war. As Turkey imported both coal and lubricants, the purpose of this policy was of course to paralyze transportation in the Ottoman Empire. Incidentally I may say the prohibition of lubricating oil caused much inconvenience to American commerce; not, however, primarily on its own account, but because of its confusion, in the minds of Greek officials, with such harmless substances as cotton seed oil and oleo. The Greek navy not only maintained a very effective blockade but also took possession of all the Aegean Islands under Turkish rule, excepting Rhodes and the Dodecanese, which Italy held as a temporary pledge for the fulfilment by Turkey of some of the conditions of the treaty by which they had closed their recent war. It will be seen, therefore, that the navy was a most important agent in the campaign, and Greece was the only one of the Allies that had a navy. The Greek navy was sufficient not only to terrorize the Turkish navy, which it reduced to complete impotence, but also to paralyze Turkish trade and commerce with the outside world, to embarrass railway transportation within the Empire, to prevent the sending of reinforcements to Macedonia or the Aegean coast of Thrace, and to detach from Turkey those Aegean Islands over which she still exercised effective jurisdiction.

SERB MILITARY OPERATIONS

On land the other Allies had been not less active than Greece. Montenegro had fired the first shot of the war. And the brave soldiers of King Nicholas, the illustrious ruler of the one Balkan state which the Turks had never conquered, were dealing deadly blows to their secular enemy both in Novi Bazar and Albania.

As the Greeks had pressed into southern Macedonia, so the Servian armies advanced through old Servia into northern and central Macedonia. In their great victory over the Turkish forces at Kumanovo they avenged the defeat of their ancestors at Kossovo five hundred years before. Still marching southward they again defeated the enemy in two great engagements, the one at Prilip and the other at Monastir. The latter city had been the object of the Greek advance to Florina, but when the prize fell to Servia, though the Greeks were appointed, it made no breach in the friendship of the two Allies. Already no doubt they were both gratified that the spheres of their military occupation were conterminous and that no Turkish territory remained for Bulgaria to occupy west of the Vardar River.

BULGARIAN MILITARY OPERATIONS

While Greece and Servia were scattering, capturing, or destroying the Turkish troops stationed in Macedonia, and closing in on that province from north and south like an irresistible vise, it fell to Bulgaria to meet the enemy's main army in the plains of Eastern Thrace. The distribution of the forces of the Allies was the natural result of their respective geographical location. Macedonia to the west of the Vardar and Bregalnitza Rivers was the only part of Turkey which adjoined Greece and Servia. Thrace, on the other hand, marched with the southern boundary of Bulgaria from the sources of the Mesta River to the Black Sea, and its eastern half was intersected diagonally by the main road from Sofia to Adrianople and Constantinople. Along this line the Bulgarians sent their forces against the common enemy as soon as war was declared. The swift story of their military exploits, the record of their brilliant victories, struck Europe with amazement. Here was a country which only thirty-five years earlier had been an unknown and despised province of Turkey in Europe now overwhelming the armies of the Ottoman Empire in the great victories of Kirk Kilisse, Lule Burgas, and Chorlu. In a few weeks the irresistible troops of King Ferdinand had reached the Chataldja line of fortifications. Only twenty-five miles beyond lay Constantinople where they hoped to celebrate their final triumph.

THE COLLAPSE OF TURKEY

The Great Powers of Europe had other views. Even if the Bulgarian delay at Chataldja--a delay probably due to exhaustion--had not given the Turks time to strengthen their defences and reorganize their forces, it is practically certain that the Bulgarian army would not have been permitted to enter Constantinople. But with the exception of the capital and its fortified fringe, all Turkey in Europe now lay at the mercy of the Allies. The entire territory was either already occupied by their troops or could be occupied at leisure. Only at three isolated points was the

Ottoman power unsubdued. The city of Adrianople, though closely besieged by the Bulgarians, still held out, and the great fortresses of Scutari in Northern Albania and Janina in Epirus remained in the hands of their Turkish garrisons.

The power of Turkey had collapsed in a few weeks. Whether the ruin was due to inefficiency and corruption in government or the injection by the Young Turk party of politics into the army or exhaustion resulting from the recent war with Italy or to other causes more obscure, we need not pause to inquire. The disaster itself, however, had spread far enough in the opinion of Europe, and a Peace Conference was summoned in December. Delegates from the belligerent states and ambassadors from the Great Powers came together in London. But their labors in the cause of peace proved unavailing. Turkey was unwilling to surrender Adrianople and Bulgaria insisted on it as a sine qua non. The Peace Conference broke up and hostilities were resumed. The siege of Adrianople was pressed by the Bulgarians with the aid of 60,000 Servian troops. It was taken by storm on March 26. Already, on March 6, Janina had yielded to the well directed attacks of King Constantine. And the fighting ended with the spectacular surrender on April 23 of Scutari to King Nicholas, who for a day at least defied the united will of Europe.

Turkey was finally compelled to accept terms of peace. In January, while the London Peace Conference was still in session, Kiamil Pasha, who had endeavored to prepare the nation for the territorial sacrifice he had all along recognized as inevitable, was driven from power and his war minister, Nazim Pasha, murdered through an uprising of the Young Turk party executed by Enver Bey, who himself demanded the resignation of Kiamil and carried it to the Sultan and secured its acceptance. The insurgents set up Mahmud Shevket Pasha as Grand Vizier and made the retention of Adrianople their cardinal policy. But the same inexorable fate overtook the new government in April as faced Kiamil in January. The Powers were insistent on peace, and the successes of the Allies left no alternative and no excuse for delay. The Young Turk party who had come to power on the Adrianople issue were accordingly compelled to ratify the cession to the allies of the city with all its mosques and tombs and historic souvenirs. The Treaty of London, which proved to be short-lived, was signed on May 30.

THE TERMS OF PEACE

The treaty of peace provided that beyond a line drawn from Enos near the mouth of the Maritza River on the Aegean Sea to Midia on the coast of the Black Sea all Turkey should be ceded to the Allies except Albania, whose boundaries were to be fixed by the Great Powers. It was also stipulated that the Great Powers should determine the destiny of the Aegean Islands belonging to Turkey which Greece now claimed by right of military occupation and the vote of their inhabitants (nearly all of whom were Greek). A more direct concession to Greece was the withdrawal of Turkish sovereignty over Crete. The treaty also contained financial and other provisions, but they do not concern us here. The essential point is that, with the exception of Constantinople and a narrow hinterland for its protection, the Moslems after more than five centuries of possession had been driven out of Europe.

This great and memorable consummation was the achievement of the united nations of the Balkans. It was not a happy augury for the immediate future to recall the historic fact that the past successes of the Moslems had been due to dissensions and divisions among their Christian neighbors.

II
THE WAR BETWEEN THE ALLIES

The Treaty of London officially eliminated Turkey from the further settlement of the Balkan question. Thanks to the good will of the Great Powers toward herself or to their rising jealousy of Bulgaria she was not stripped of her entire European possessions west of the Chataldja lines where the victorious Bulgarians had planted their standards. The Enos-Midia frontier not only guaranteed to her a considerable portion of territory which the Bulgarians had occupied but extended her coast line, from the point where the Chataldja lines strike the Sea of Marmora, out through the Dardanelles and along the Aegean littoral to the mouth of the Maritza River. To that extent the Great Powers may be said to have re-established the Turks once more in Europe from which they had been practically driven by the Balkan Allies and especially the Bulgarians. All the rest of her European possessions, however, Turkey was forced to surrender either in trust to the Great Powers or absolutely to the Balkan Allies.

The great question now was how the Allies should divide among themselves the spoils of war.

RIVAL AMBITIONS OF THE ALLIES

This was a difficult matter to adjust. Before the war began, as we have already seen, a Treaty of Partition had been negotiated between Bulgaria and Servia, but conditions had changed materially in the interval and Servia now demanded a revision of the treaty and refused to withdraw her troops from Central Macedonia, which the treaty had marked for reversion to Bulgaria. In consequence the relations between the governments and peoples of Servia and Bulgaria were dangerously strained. The Bulgarians denounced the Servians as perfidious and faithless and the Servians responded by excoriating the colossal greed and intolerance of the Bulgarians. The immemorial mutual hatred of the two Slav nations was stirred to its lowest depths, and it boiled and sputtered like a witches' cauldron.

In Eastern Macedonia Bulgarians and Greeks were each eagerly pushing their respective spheres of occupation without much regard to the rights or feeling of the other Ally. Though the Bulgarians had not forgiven the Greeks for anticipating them in the capture of Saloniki in the month of November, the rivalry between them in the following winter and spring had for its stage the territory between the Struma and the Mesta Rivers--and especially the quadrilateral marked by Kavala and Orphani on the coast and Seres and Drama on the line of railway from Saloniki to Adrianople. They had one advantage over the Bulgarians: their troops could be employed to secure extensions of territory for the Hellenic kingdom at a time when Bulgaria still needed the bulk of her forces to fight the Turks at Chataldja and Adrianople. Hence the Greeks occupied towns in the district from which Bulgarian troops had been recalled. Nor did they hesitate to dislodge scattered Bulgarian troops which their ally had left behind to establish a claim of occupation. Naturally disputes arose between the military commanders and these led to repeated armed encounters. On March 5 Greeks and Bulgarians fought at Nigrita as they subsequently fought at Pravishta, Leftera, Panghaion, and Anghista.

This conduct of the Allies toward one another while the common enemy was still in the field boded ill for their future relations. "Our next war will be with Bulgaria," said the man on the street in Athens, and this bellicose sentiment was reciprocated alike by the Bulgarian people and the Bulgarian army. The secular mutual enmities and animosities of the Greeks and Bulgarians, which self-interest had suppressed long enough to enable the Balkan Allies to make European Turkey their own, burst forth with redoubled violence under the stimulus of the imperious demand which the occasion now made upon them all for an equitable distribution of the conquered territory. For ages the fatal vice of the Balkan nations has been the immoderate and intolerant assertion by each of its own claims coupled with contemptuous disregard of the rights of others.

ALBANIA A CAUSE OF FRICTION

There were also external causes which contributed to the deepening tragedy in the Balkans. Undoubtedly the most potent was the dislocation of the plans of the Allies by the creation of an independent Albania. This new kingdom was called into being by the voice of the European concert at the demand of Austria-Hungary supported by Italy.

The controlling force in politics, though not the only force, is self-interest. Austria-Hungary had long sought an outlet through Macedonia to the Aegean by way of Saloniki. It was also the aim of Servia to reach the Adriatic. But the foreign policy of Austria-Hungary, which has millions of Serbs under its dominion, has steadily opposed the aggrandizement of Servia. And now that Servia and her allies had taken possession of Macedonia and blocked the path of Austria-Hungary to Saloniki, it was not merely revenge, it was self-interest pursuing a consistent foreign policy, which moved the Dual Monarchy to make the cardinal feature of its Balkan programme the exclusion of Servia from access to the Adriatic Sea. Before the first Balkan war began the Adriatic littoral was under the dominion of Austria-Hungary and Italy, for though Montenegro and European Turkey were their maritime neighbors neither of them had any naval strength. Naturally these two dominant powers desired that after the close of the Balkan war they should not be in a worse position in the Adriatic than heretofore. But if Servia were allowed to expand westward to the Adriatic, their supremacy might in the future be challenged. For Servia might enter into special relations with her great sister Slav state, Russia, or a confederation might be formed embracing all the Balkan states between the Black Sea and the Adriatic: and, in either event, Austria-Hungary and Italy would no longer enjoy the unchallenged supremacy on the Adriatic coasts which was theirs so long as Turkey held dominion over the maritime country lying between Greece and Montenegro. As a necessity of practical politics, therefore, there emerged the Austro-Italian policy of an independent Albania. But natural and essential as this policy was for Italy and Austria-Hungary, it was fatal to Servia's dream of expansion to the Adriatic; it set narrow limits to the northward extension of Greece into Epirus, and the southward extension of Montenegro below Scutari; it impelled these Allies to seek compensation in territory that Bulgaria had regarded as her peculiar preserve; and as a consequence it seriously menaced the existence of the Balkan Alliance torn as it already was by mutual jealousies, enmities, aggressions, and recriminations.

RECOIL OF SERVIA TOWARD THE AEGEAN

The first effect of the European fiat regarding an independent Albania was the recoil of Servia against Bulgaria. Confronted by the force majeure of the Great Powers which estopped her advance to the Adriatic, Servia turned her anxious regard toward the Gulf of Saloniki and the Aegean Sea. Already her victorious armies had occupied Macedonia from the Albanian frontier eastward beyond the Vardar River to Strumnitza, Istib, and Kochana, and southward below Monastir and Ghevgheli, where they touched the boundary of the Greek occupation of Southern Macedonia. An agreement with the Greeks, who held the city of Saloniki and its hinterland as well as the whole Chalcidician Peninsula, would ensure Servia an outlet to the sea. And the merchants of Saloniki--mostly the descendants of Jews expelled from Spain in the fifteenth century--were shrewd enough to recognize the advantage to their city of securing the commerce of Servia, especially as they were destined to lose, in consequence of hostile tariffs certain to be established by the conquerors, a considerable portion of the trade which had formerly flowed to them without let or hindrance from a large section of European Turkey. The government of Greece was equally favorably disposed to this programme; for, in the first place, it was to its interest to cultivate friendly relations with Servia, in view of possible embroilments with Bulgaria; and, in the second place, it had to countercheck the game of those who wanted either to make Saloniki a free city or to incorporate it in a Big Bulgaria, and who were using with some effect the argument that the annexation of the city to Greece meant the throttling of its trade and the annihilation of its prosperity. The interests of the city of Saloniki, the interests of Greece, and the interests of Servia all combined to demand the free flow of Servian trade by way of Saloniki. And if no other power obtained jurisdiction over any Macedonian territory through which that trade passed, it would be easy for the Greek and Servian governments to come to an understanding.

TREATY RESTRICTIONS

Just here, however, was the rub. The secret treaty of March, 1912, providing for the offensive and defensive alliance of Bulgaria and Servia against the Ottoman Empire regulated, in case of victory, the division of the conquered territory between the Allies. And the extreme limit, on the south and east, of Turkish territory assigned to Servia by this treaty was fixed by a line starting from Ochrida on the borders of Albania and running northeastward across the Vardar River a few miles above Veles and thence, following the same general direction, through Ovcepolje and Egri Palanka to Golema Vreh on the frontier of Bulgaria--a terminus some twenty miles southeast of the meeting point of Servia, Macedonia, and Bulgaria. During the war with Turkey the Servian armies had paid no attention to the Ochrida-Golema Vreh line. The great victory over the Turks at Kumanovo, by which the Slav defeat at Kossovo five hundred years earlier was avenged, was, it is true, won at a point north of the line in question. But the subsequent victories of Prilip and Monastir were gained to the south of it--far, indeed, into the heart of the Macedonian territory recognized by the treaty as Bulgarian.

If you look at a map you will see that the boundary between Servia and Bulgaria, starting from the Danube, runs in a slightly undulating line due south. Now what the military forces of King Peter did during the war of the Balkan states with the Ottoman Empire was to occupy all European Turkey south of Servia between the prolongation of that boundary line and the new Kingdom of Albania till they met the Hellenic army advancing northward under Crown Prince Constantine, when the two governments agreed on a common boundary for New Servia and New Greece along a line starting from Lake Presba and running eastward between Monastir and Florina to the Vardar River a little to the south of Ghevgheli.

THE APPLE OF DISCORD

But this arrangement between Greece and Servia would leave no territory for Bulgaria in Central and Western Macedonia! Yet Servia had solemnly bound herself by treaty not to ask for any Turkish territory below the Ochrida-Golema Vreh line. There was no similar treaty with Greece, but Bulgaria regarded the northern frontier of New Greece as a matter for adjustment between the two governments. Servia, withdrawn behind the Ochrida-Golema Vreh line in accordance with the terms of the treaty, would at any rate have nothing to say about the matter. And, although the Bulgarian government never communicated, officially or unofficially, its own views to Greece or Servia, I believe we should not make much mistake in asserting that a line drawn from Ochrida to Saloniki (which Bulgaria in spite of the Greek occupation continued to claim) would roughly represent the limit of its voluntary concession. Now if you imagine a base line drawn from Saloniki to Golema Vreh, you have an equilateral triangle resting on Ochrida as apex. And this equilateral triangle represents approximately what Bulgaria claimed in the western half of Macedonia as her own.

The war between the Allies was fought over the possession of this triangle. The larger portion of it had in the war against Turkey been occupied by the forces of Servia; and the nation, inflamed by the military spirit of the army, had made up its mind that, treaty or no treaty, it should not be evacuated. On the south, especially above Vodena, the Greeks had occupied a section of the fatal triangle. And the two governments had decided that they would not tolerate the driving of a Bulgarian wedge between New Servia and New Greece. Bulgaria, on the other hand, was inexorable in her demands on Servia for the fulfilment of the terms of the Treaty of Partition. At the same time she worried the Greek government about the future of Saloniki, and that at a time when the Greek people were criticizing Mr. Venizelos for having allowed the Bulgarians to occupy regions in Macedonia and Thrace inhabited by Greeks, notably Seres, Drama, and Kavala, and the adjacent country between the Struma and the Mesta. These were additional causes of dissension between the Allies. But the primary disruptive force was the attraction, the incompatible attraction, exerted on them all by that central Macedonian triangle whose apex rested on the ruins of Czar Samuel's palace at Ochrida and whose base extended from Saloniki to Golema Vreh.

THE CLAIM OF BULGARIA

From that base line to the Black Sea nearly all European Turkey (with the exception of the Chalcidician Peninsula, including Saloniki and its hinterland) had been occupied by the military forces of Bulgaria. Why then was Bulgaria so insistent on getting beyond that base line, crossing the Vardar, and possessing herself of Central Macedonia up to Ochrida and the eastern frontier of Albania?

The answer, in brief, is that it has been the undeviating policy of Bulgaria, ever since her own emancipation by Russia in 1877, to free the Bulgarians still under the Ottoman yoke and unite them in a common fatherland. The Great Bulgaria which was created by Russia in the treaty she forced on Turkey--the Treaty of San Stefano--was constructed under the influence of the idea of a union of the Bulgarian race in a single state under a common government. This treaty was afterward torn to pieces by the Congress of Berlin, which set up for the Bulgarians a very diminutive principality. But the Bulgarians, from the palace down to the meanest hut, have always been animated by that racial and national idea. The annexation of Eastern Roumelia in 1885 was a great step in the direction of its realization. And it was to carry that programme to completion that Bulgaria made war against Turkey in 1912. Her primary object was the liberation of the Bulgarians in Macedonia and their incorporation in a Great Bulgaria. And the Treaty of Partition with Servia seemed, in the event of victory over Turkey, to afford a guarantee of the accomplishment of her long-cherished purpose. It was a strange irony of fate that while as a result of the geographical situation of the belligerents Bulgaria, at the close of the war with Turkey, found herself in actual occupation of all European Turkey from the Black Sea up to the River Struma and beyond,--that is, all Thrace to Chataldja as well as Eastern Macedonia--her allies were in possession of the bulk of Macedonia, including the entire triangle she had planned to inject between the frontiers of New Servia and New Greece!

The Bulgarians claimed this triangle on ethnological grounds. Its inhabitants, they asseverated, were their brethren, as genuinely Bulgarian as the subjects of King Ferdinand.

RACIAL PROPAGANDA IN MACEDONIA

Of all perplexing subjects in the world few can be more baffling than the distribution of races in Macedonia. The Turks classify the population, not by language or by physical characteristics, but by religion. A Greek is a member of the Orthodox Church who recognizes the patriarch of Constantinople; a Bulgarian, on the other hand, is one of the same religious faith who recognizes the exarch; and since the Servians in Turkey have no independent church but recognize the patriarchate they are often, as opposed to Bulgarians, called Greeks. Race, being thus merged in religion--in something that rests on the human will and not on physical characteristics fixed by nature--can in that part of the world be changed as easily as religion. A Macedonian may be a Greek to-day, a Bulgarian to-morrow, and a Servian next day. We have all heard of the captain in the comic opera who "in spite of all temptations to belong to other nations" remained an Englishman. There would have been nothing comic in this assertion had the redoubtable captain lived in Macedonia. In that land a race is a political party composed of members with common customs and religion who stand for a "national idea" which they strenuously endeavor to force on others.

Macedonia is the land of such racial propaganda. As the Turkish government forbids public meetings for political purposes, the propaganda takes an ecclesiastical and linguistic form. Each "race" seeks to convert the people to its faith by the agency of schools and churches, which teach and use its own language. Up to the middle of the nineteenth century the Greeks, owing to their privileged ecclesiastical position in the Ottoman Empire, had exclusive spiritual and educational jurisdiction over the members of the Orthodox Church in Macedonia. The opposition of the Bulgarians led, as we have already seen, to the establishment in 1870 of the exarchate, that is, of an independent Bulgarian Orthodox Church with the exarch at its head. The Bulgarian propaganda in Macedonia demanded the appointment of bishops to conduct churches and schools under the authority of the exarchate. In 1891 the Porte conceded Bulgarian bishops to Ochrida and Uskub, in 1894 to Veles and Nevrokop, and in 1898 to Monastir, Strumnitza, and Dibra. As has been well said, the church of the exarchate was really occupied in creating Bulgarians: it offered to the Slavonic population of Macedonia services and schools conducted in a language which they understood and showed a genuine interest in their education. By 1900 Macedonia had 785 Bulgarian schools, 39,892 pupils, and 1,250 teachers.

The Servian propaganda in Macedonia was at a disadvantage in comparison with the Bulgarian because it had not a separate ecclesiastical organization. As we have already seen, the orthodox Serbs owe allegiance to the Greek patriarch in Constantinople. And at first they did not push their propaganda as zealously or as successfully as the Bulgarians. In fact the national aspirations of the people of Servia had been in the direction of Bosnia and Herzegovina; but after these provinces were assigned to Austria by the Treaty of Berlin, a marked change of attitude occurred in the Servian government and nation. They now claimed as Servian the Slavonic population of Macedonia which hitherto Bulgaria had cultivated as her own. The course of politics in Bulgaria, notably her embroilment with Russia, inured to the advantage of the Servian propaganda in Macedonia, which after 1890 made great headway. The Servian government made liberal contributions for Macedonian schools. And before the nineteenth century closed the Servian propaganda could claim 178 schools in the vilayets of Saloniki and Monastir and in Uskub with 321 teachers and 7,200 pupils.

These Slav propagandists made serious encroachments upon the Greek cause, which, only a generation earlier, had possessed a practical monopoly in Macedonia. Greek efforts too were for a time almost paralyzed in consequence of the disastrous issue of the Greco-Turkish war in 1897. Nevertheless in 1901 the Greeks claimed 927 schools in the vilayets of Saloniki and Monastir with 1,397 teachers and 57,607 pupils.

RACIAL FACTS AND FALLACIES

The more bishops, churches, and schools a nationality could show, the stronger its claim on the reversion of Macedonia when the Turk should be driven out of Europe! There was no doubt much juggling with statistics. And though schools and churches were provided by Greeks, Servians, and Bulgarians to satisfy the spiritual and intellectual needs of their kinsmen in Macedonia, there was always the ulterior (which was generally the dominant) object of staking out claims in the domain soon to drop from the paralyzed hand of the Turk. The bishops may have been good shepherds of their flocks, but the primary qualification for the office was, I imagine, the gift of aggressive political leadership. The Turkish government now favored one nationality and now another as the interests of the moment seemed to suggest. With an impish delight in playing off Slav against Greek and Servian against Bulgarian, its action on applications for bishoprics was generally taken with a view to embarrassing the rival Christian nationalities. And it could when necessary keep the propagandists within severe limits. The Bulgarians grew bold after securing so many bishoprics in the nineties and the bishop at Uskub thought to open new schools and churches. But the Turkish governor--the Vali--summoned him and delivered this warning: "O Bulgarian, sit upon the eggs you have, and do not burst your belly by trying to lay more."

How are we to determine the racial complexion of a country in which race is certified by religion, in which religion is measured by the number of bishops and churches and schools, in which bishops and churches and schools are created and maintained by a propaganda conducted by competing external powers, and in which the results of the propaganda are determined largely by money and men sent from Sofia, Athens, and Belgrade, subject always to the caprice and manipulation of the Sultan's government at Constantinople?

In Southern Macedonia from the Thessalian frontier as far north as the parallel of Saloniki, the population is almost exclusively Greek, as is also the whole of the Chalcidician Peninsula, while further east the coast region between the Struma and the Mesta is also predominantly Greek. Eastern Macedonia to the north of the line of Seres and Drama and south of the Kingdom of Bulgaria is generally Bulgarian. On the northwest from the city of Uskub up to the confines of Servia and Bosnia, Macedonia is mixed Serb, Bulgarian, and Albanian, with the Serb element preponderating as you travel northward and the Albanian westward.

PERSONAL OBSERVATIONS AND EXPERIENCES

The difficulty comes when we attempt to give the racial character of Central Macedonia, which is equally remote from Greece, Bulgaria, and Servia. I travelled through this district last summer. On June 29, when the war broke out between the Allies I found myself in Uskub. Through the courtesy of the Servian authorities I was permitted to ride on the first military train which left the city. Descending at Veles I drove across Central Macedonia by way of Prilip to Monastir, spending the first night, for lack of a better bed, in the carriage, which was guarded by Servian sentries. From Monastir I motored over execrable roads to Lake Presba and Lake Ochrida and thence beyond the city of Ochrida to Struga on the Black Drin, from which I looked out on the mountains of Albania.

Coming from Athens where for many months I had listened to patriotic stories of the thorough permeation of Macedonia by Greek settlements my first surprise was my inability to discover a Greek majority in Central Macedonia. In most of the cities a fraction of the population indeed is Greek and as a rule the colony is prosperous. This is especially true in Monastir, which is a stronghold of Greek influence. But while half the population of Monastir is Mohammedan the so-called Bulgarians form the majority of the Christian population, though both Servians and Roumanians have conducted energetic propaganda. In Veles two-thirds of the population are Christians and nearly all of these are called Bulgarians. In Ochrida the lower town is Mohammedan and the upper Christian, and the Christian population is almost exclusively of the Bulgarian Church.

It does not follow, however, that the people of Central Macedonia, even if Bulgarian churches are in the ascendant among them, are really connected by ties of blood and language with Bulgaria rather than with Servia. If history is invoked we shall have to admit that under Dushan this region was a part of the Serb empire as under Simeon and Asen it was part of the Bulgarian. If an appeal is made to anthropology the answer is still uncertain. For while the Mongolian features--broad flat faces, narrow eyes, and straight black hair--which characterize the subjects of King Ferdinand can be seen--I myself have seen them--as far west as Ochrida, they may also be found all over Northern Servia as far as Belgrade though the Servian physical type is entirely different. There is no fixed connection between the anthropological unit and the linguistic or political unit. Furthermore, while there are well-marked groups who call themselves Serbs or Bulgarians there is a larger population not so clearly differentiated by physique or language. Undoubtedly they are Slavs. But whether Serb or Bulgarian, or intermediate between the two, no one to-day can demonstrate. Central Macedonia has its own dialects, any one of which under happy literary auspices might have developed into a separate language. And the men who speak them to-day can more or less understand either Servian or Bulgarian. Hence as the anonymous and highly authoritative author of "Turkey in Europe," who calls himself Odysseus, declares:

"The practical conclusion is that neither Greeks, Servians, nor Bulgarians have a right to claim Central Macedonia. The fact that they all do so shows how weak each claim must be."

Yet it was Bulgaria's intransigent assertion of her claim to Central Macedonia which led to the war between the Allies.

It will be instructive to consider the attitude of each of the governments concerned on the eve of the conflict. I hope I am in a position correctly to report it. Certainly I had unusual opportunities to learn it. For besides the official position I held in Athens during the entire course of both Balkan wars I visited the Balkan states in June and was accorded the privilege of discussing the then pending crisis with the prime ministers of Roumania, Servia, and Bulgaria. It would of course be improper to quote them; nay more, I feel myself under special obligation sacredly to respect the confidence they reposed in me. But the frank disclosures they made in these conversations gave me a point of view for the comprehension of the situation and the estimate of facts which I have found simply invaluable. And if Mr. Venizelos in Athens, or Mr. Maioresco in Bukarest, or Mr. Pashitch in Belgrade, or Dr. Daneff, who is no longer prime minister of Bulgaria, should ever chance to read what I am saying, I hope each will feel that I have fairly and impartially presented the attitude which their respective governments had taken at this critical moment on the vital issue then confronting them.

THE ATTITUDE OF SERVIA

I have already indicated the situation of Servia. Compelled by the Great Powers to withdraw her troops from Albania, after they had triumphantly made their way to the Adriatic, she was now requested by Bulgaria to evacuate Central Macedonia up to the Ochrida-Golema Vreh line in accordance with the terms of the treaty between the two countries which was ratified in March, 1912. The Servian government believed that for the loss of Albania, which the treaty assumed would be annexed to Servia, they were entitled to compensation in Macedonia. And if now, instead of compensation for the loss of an outlet on the Adriatic, they were to withdraw their forces from Central Macedonia and allow Bulgaria to establish herself between New Servia and New Greece, they would block their own way to Saloniki, which was the only prospect now left of a Servian outlet to the sea. Nor was this the whole story by any means. The army, which comprised all able-bodied Servians, was in possession of Central Macedonia; and the military leaders, with the usual professional bias in favor of imperialism, dictated their expansionist views to the government at Belgrade. If Bulgaria would not voluntarily grant compensation for the loss of Albania, the Servian people were ready to take it by force. They had also a direct claim against Bulgaria. They had sent 60,000 soldiers to the siege of Adrianople, which the Bulgarians had hitherto failed to capture. And the Servians were now asking, in bitter irony, whether they had gone to war solely for the benefit of Bulgaria; whether besides helping her to win all Thrace and Eastern Macedonia they were now to present her with Central Macedonia, and that at a time when the European Concert had stripped them of the expected prize of Albania with its much desired Adriatic littoral! This argument was graphically presented on a map of which I secured a copy in Belgrade. The legend on this map reads as follows:

"Territories occupied by Servia 55,000 square miles. Servia cedes to her allies in the east and south 3,800 square miles. Servia cedes to Albania 15,200 square miles. Servia retains 36,000 square miles. Territories occupied by Bulgaria to Enos-Midia, 51,200 square miles. The Bulgarians demand from the Servians still 10,240 square miles. According to Bulgarian pretensions Bulgaria should get

61,520 square miles and Servia only 25,760!"

PROPOSED REVISION OF TREATY AND ARBITRATION

When the treaty between Servia and Bulgaria was negotiated, it seems to have been assumed that the theatre of a war with Turkey would be Macedonia and that Thrace--the country from the Mesta to the Black Sea--would remain intact to Turkey. And if the rest of Turkey in Europe up to the Adriatic were conquered by the two Allies, the Ochrida-Golema Vreh line would make a fairly equitable division between them of the spoils of war. But with Albania denied to Servia and Thrace occupied by Bulgaria, conditions had wholly changed. The Servian government declared that the changed conditions had abrogated the Treaty of Partition and that it was for the two governments now to adjust themselves to the logic of events! On May 28 Mr. Pashitch, the Servian prime minister, formally demanded a revision of the treaty. A personal interview with the Bulgarian prime minister, Mr. Gueshoff, followed on June 2 at Tsaribrod. And Mr. Gueshoff accepted Mr. Pashitch's suggestion (which originated with Mr. Venizelos, the Greek prime minister) of a conference of representatives of the four Allies at St. Petersburg. For it should be added that, in the Treaty of Partition, the Czar had been named as arbiter in case of any territorial dispute between the two parties.

What followed in the next few days has never been clearly disclosed. But it was of transcendent importance. I have always thought that if Mr. Gueshoff, one of the authors of the Balkan Alliance, had been allowed like Mr. Venizelos and Mr. Pashitch, to finish his work, there would have been no war between the Allies. I did not enjoy the personal acquaintance of Mr. Gueshoff, but I regarded him as a wise statesman of moderate views, who was disposed to make reasonable concessions for the sake of peace. But a whole nation in arms, flushed with the sense of victory, is always dangerous to the authority of civil government. If Mr. Gueshoff was ready to arrange some accommodation with Mr. Pashitch, the military party in Bulgaria was all the more insistent in its demands on Servia for the evacuation of Central Macedonia. Even in Servia Mr. Pashitch had great difficulty in repressing the jingo ardor of the army, whose bellicose spirit was believed to find expression in the attitude of the Crown Prince. But the provocation in Bulgaria was greater, because, when all was said and done, Servia was actually violating an agreement with Bulgaria to which she had solemnly set her name. Possibly the military party gained the ear of King Ferdinand. Certainly it was reported that he was consulting with leaders of the opposition. Presumably they were all dissatisfied with the conciliatory attitude which Mr. Gueshoff had shown in the Tsaribrod conference. Whatever the explanation, Mr. Gueshoff resigned on June 9.

DELAY AND OPPOSITION OF BULGARIA

On that very day the Czar summoned the Kings of Bulgaria and Servia to submit their disputes to his decision. While this demand was based on a specific provision of the Servo-Bulgarian treaty, His Majesty also urged it on the ground of devotion to the Slav cause. This pro-Slav argument provoked much criticism in Austro-Hungarian circles which resented bitterly the assumption of Slav hegemony in Balkan affairs. However, on June 12 Bulgaria and Servia accepted Russian arbitration. But the terms were not agreed upon. While Mr. Venizelos and Mr. Pashitch impatiently awaited the summons to St. Petersburg they could get no definite information of the intentions of the Bulgarian government. And the rivalry of Austria-Hungary and Russia for predominance in the Balkans was never more intense than at this critical moment.

On June 14 Dr. Daneff was appointed prime minister in succession to Mr. Gueshoff. He had represented Bulgaria in the London Peace Conference where his aggressive and uncompromising attitude had perturbed his fellow delegates from the other Balkan states and provoked some criticism in the European press. He was known as a Russophil. And he seems now to have got assurance from Russia that she would maintain the Bulgarian view of the treaty with Servia, although she had at one time favored the Servian demand for an extensive revision of it. Certainly Dr. Daneff voiced the views and sentiments of the Bulgarian army and nation. I was in Sofia the week before the outbreak of the war between the Allies. And the two points on which everybody insisted were, first, that Servia must be compelled to observe the Treaty of Partition, and, secondly, that Central Macedonia must be annexed to Bulgaria. For these things all Bulgarians were ready to fight. And flushed with their great victories over the main army of Turkey they believed it would be an easy task to overpower the forces of Servia and Greece. For the Greeks they entertained a sort of contempt; and as for the Servians, had they not already defeated them completely at Slivnitza in 1886? Men high in the military service of the nation assured me that the Bulgarian army would be in Belgrade in eight days after war was declared. The Greeks too would quickly be driven out of Saloniki. The idea of a conference to decide the territorial question in dispute between the Allies found no favor in any quarter.

Now it is important that full justice should be done to Bulgaria. As against Servia, if Servia had stood alone, she might have appealed to the sanctity and inviolability of treaties. Circumstances had indeed changed since the treaty was negotiated. But was that a good reason, Bulgaria might have asked, why she should be excluded from Central Macedonia which the treaty guaranteed to her? Was that a good reason why she should not emancipate her Macedonian brethren for whose sake she had waged a bloody and costly war with Turkey? The Bulgarians saw nothing in the problem but their treaty with Servia and apparently cared for no territorial compensation without Central Macedonia.

BULGARIA'S UNCOMPROMISING POLICY

The Bulgarians were blind to all facts and considerations but the abstract terms of the treaty with Servia. It was a fact, however, that the war against Turkey had been fought by four Allies. It was a fact that the Ottoman government had ceded European Turkey (except Albania) to these four Allies. No two of the Allies could divide between themselves the common possession. A division made by the four Allies might contravene the terms of a treaty which existed between any two of the Allies prior to the outbreak of the war. In any event it was for the four Allies together to effect a distribution of the territory ceded to them by Turkey. For that purpose a conference was an essential organ. How otherwise could the four nations reach any agreement? Yet the Bulgarians--army, government, and nation--were obsessed by the fixed idea that Bulgaria enjoyed not only a primacy in this matter but a sort of sovereign monopoly by virtue of which it was her right and privilege to determine how much of the common spoils she should assign Servia (with whom she had an ante-bellum treaty), and, after Servia had been eliminated, how much she could spare to Greece (with whom no treaty of partition existed), and, when Greece had been disposed of, whether any crumbs could be flung to Montenegro, who had indeed very little to hope for from the Bulgarian government. And so Bulgaria opposed a conference of the four prime ministers though a conference was the natural, obvious, and necessary method of disposing of the common business pressing upon them.

The attitude of Bulgaria left no alternative but war. Yet the Bulgarian government failed to reckon the cost of war. Was it not madness for Bulgaria to force war upon Greece, Servia, and Montenegro on the west at a time when Roumania was making demands for territorial compensation on the north and Turkey was sure to seize the occasion to win back territory which Bulgaria had just wrested from her on the south? Never was a government blinder to the significant facts of a critical situation. All circumstances conspired to prescribe peace as the manifest policy for Bulgaria, yet nearly every step taken by the government was provocative of war. The Bulgarian army had covered itself with glory in the victorious campaign against the Moslem. A large part of European Turkey was already in Bulgarian hands. To imperil that glory and those possessions by the risk of a new war, when the country was exhausted and new enemies lay in wait, was as foolish as it was criminal. That way madness lay. Yet that way the policy pursued by the Bulgarian government infallibly led. Must we assume that there is some ground for suspecting that Austria-Hungary was inciting Bulgaria to war? We must leave it to history to answer. If the result was a terrible disaster, that was only the old Greek Nemesis of the gods for the outraged principles of reason and moderation.

THE CONCILIATORY SPIRIT OF GREECE

Those principles, thanks to the conciliatory spirit of Mr. Venizelos, the prime minister, and the steady support of King Constantine, who was also commander-in-chief, were loyally followed in Greece. A few days after the declaration of war against the Ottoman Empire, into which Greece was precipitately hastened by the unexpected action of Servia and Bulgaria, the Greek foreign minister addressed a communication to the Allies on the subject of the division of conquered territory. He traced the line of Greek claims, as based on ethnological grounds, and added that, as he foresaw difficulties in the way of a direct adjustment, he thought the disputed points should be submitted to arbitration. But months followed months without bringing from Bulgaria any clear reply to this just and reasonable proposal of the Greek government. Nevertheless, Mr. Venizelos persisted in his attitude of conciliation toward Bulgaria. He made concessions, not only in Thrace but in Eastern Macedonia, for which he was bitterly criticized on the ground of sacrificing vital Greek interests to Bulgaria. He recognized, as his critics refused to do, that the Balkan question could not be settled on ethnological principles alone; one had to take account also of geographical necessities. He saw that the Greeks in Thrace must be handed over to Bulgaria. He demanded only the Macedonian territory which the Greek forces had actually occupied, including Saloniki with an adequate hinterland. As the attitude of Bulgaria became more uncompromising, as she pushed her army of occupation further westward, Mr. Venizelos was even ready to make the River Struma the eastern boundary of New Greece, and to abandon to Bulgaria the Aegean littoral between the Struma and the Mesta Rivers including Greek cities like Kavala, Seres, and Drama. But these new concessions of Mr. Venizelos were in danger of alienating from him the support of the Greek nation without yielding anything in return from Bulgaria. The outbreak of the war between the Allies saved him from a difficult political position. Yet against that war Mr. Venizelos strove resolutely to the end. And when in despite of all his efforts war came, he was justified in saying, as he did say to the national parliament, that the Greeks had the right to present themselves before the civilized world with head erect because this new war which was bathing with blood the Balkan Peninsula had not been provoked by Greece or brought about by the demand of Greece to receive satisfaction for all her ethnological claims. And this position in which he had placed his country was, he proudly declared, a "moral capital" of the greatest value.

BULGARIA BEGINS HOSTILITIES

Bulgaria's belated acceptance of Russian arbitration was not destined to establish peace. Yet Dr. Daneff, the prime minister, who received me on June 27 and talked freely of the Balkan situation (perhaps the more freely because in this conversation it transpired that we had been fellow students together at the University of Heidelberg), decided on June 28 not to go to war with the Allies. Yet that very evening at eight o'clock, unknown to Dr. Daneff, an order in cipher and marked "very urgent" was issued by General Savoff to the commander of the fourth army directing him on the following evening to attack the Servians "most vigorously along the whole front." On the following afternoon, the 29th, General Savoff issued another order to the army commanders giving further instructions for attacks on the Servians and Greeks, including an attack on Saloniki, stating that these attacks were taking place "without any official declaration of war," and that they were undertaken in order to accustom the Bulgarian army to regard their former allies as enemies, to hasten the activities of the Russian government, to compel the former allies to be more conciliatory, and to secure new territories for Bulgaria! Who was responsible for this deplorable lack of harmony between the civil government and the military authorities has not yet been officially disclosed. Did General Savoff act on his own responsibility? Or is there any truth in the charge that King Ferdinand after a long consultation with the Austro-Hungarian Minister instructed the General to issue the order? Dr. Daneff knew nothing of it, and though he made every effort to stop the resulting hostilities, the dogs of war had been let loose and could not now be torn from one another's throats.

There had been sporadic fighting in Macedonia between the Allies for some months past. Greece and Servia had concluded an anti-Bulgarian alliance on June 1. They also entered into a convention with Roumania by which that power agreed to intervene in case of war between the late Allies. And war having been declared, Roumania seized Silistria at midnight, July 10. Meanwhile the Servian and Greek forces were fighting the Bulgarians hard at Kilkis, Doiran, and other points between the Vardar and the Struma. And, as if Bulgaria had not enemies enough on her back already, the Turkish Army on July 12 left the Chataldja fortifications, crossed the Enos-Midia line, and in less than two weeks, with Enver Bey at its head, reoccupied Adrianople. Bulgaria was powerless to stop the further advance of the Turks, nor had she forces to send against the Roumanians who marched unopposed through the neighboring country till Sofia itself was within their power.

No nation could stand up against such fearful odds. Dr. Daneff resigned on July 15. And the new ministry had to make the best terms it could.

TERMS OF PEACE

A Peace Conference met at Bukarest on July 28, and peace was signed on August 10. By this Treaty of Bukarest Servia secured not only all that part of Macedonia already under her occupation but gained also an eastward extension beyond the Doiran-Istib-Kochana line into purely Bulgarian territory. Greece fared still better under the treaty; for it gave her not only all the Macedonian lands she had already occupied but extended her domain on the Aegean littoral as far east as the mouth of the Mesta and away into the interior as far above Seres and Drama as they are from the sea,--thus establishing the northern frontier of New Greece from Lake Presba (near the eastern boundary of Albania) on a northward-ascending line past Ghevgheli and Doiran to Kainchal in Thrace on the other side of the Mesta River. This assignment of territory conquered from Turkey had the effect of shutting out Bulgaria from the Western Aegean; and the littoral left to Bulgaria between the Mesta River and the Turkish boundary has no harbor of any consequence but Dedeagach, which is much inferior to Kavala.

The new Turkish boundary was arranged by negotiations between the Bulgarian and Ottoman governments. The terminus on the Black Sea was pushed north from Midia almost up to the southern boundary of Bulgaria. Enos remained the terminus on the Aegean. But the two termini were connected by a curved line which after following the Maritza River to a point between Sufli and Dimotika then swung in a semicircle well beyond Adrianople to Bulgaria and the Black Sea. Thus Bulgaria was compelled to cede back to the Asiatic enemy not only Adrianople but the battlefields of Kirk Kilisse, Lule Burgas, and Chorlu on which her brave soldiers had won such magnificent victories over the Moslems.

THE ATTITUDE OF ROUMANIA

The Treaty of Bukarest marked the predominance of Roumania in Balkan affairs. And of course Roumania had her own reward. She had long coveted the northeastern corner of Bulgaria, from Turtukai on the Danube to Baltchik on the Black Sea. And this territory, even some miles beyond that line, Bulgaria was now compelled to cede to her by the treaty. It is a fertile area with a population of some 300,000 souls, many of whom are Turks.

The claim of Roumania to compensation for her neutrality during the first Balkan war was severely criticized by the independent press of western Europe. It was first put forward in the London Peace Conference, but rejected by Dr. Daneff, the Bulgarian delegate. But the Roumanian government persisted in pressing the claim, and the Powers finally decided to mediate, with the result that the city of Silistria and the immediately adjoining territory were assigned to Roumania. Neither state was satisfied with the award and the second Balkan war broke out before the transfer had been effected. This gave Roumania the opportunity to enforce her original claim, and, despite the advice of Austria-Hungary, she used it, as we have already seen.

The Roumanian government justifies its position in this matter by two considerations. In the first place, as Roumania was larger and more populous than any of the Balkan states, the Roumanian nation could not sit still with folded arms while Bulgaria wrested this preeminence from her. And if Bulgaria had not precipitated a war among the Allies, if she had been content with annexing the portion of European Turkey which she held under military occupation, New Bulgaria would have contained a greater area and a larger population than Roumania. The Roumanians claim, accordingly, that the course they pursued was dictated by a legitimate and vital national interest. And, in the second place, as Greeks, Servians, and Bulgarians based their respective claims to Macedonian territory on the racial character of the inhabitants, Roumania asserted that the presence of a large Roumanian (or Vlach) population in that disputed region gave her an equally valid claim to a share in the common estate.

In all Macedonia there may be some 100,000 Vlachs, though Roumanian officials put the number much higher. Many of them are highland shepherds; others engage in transportation with trains of horses or mules; those in the lowlands are good farmers. They are found especially in the mountains and valleys between Thessaly and Albania. They are generally favorable to the Greek cause. Most of them speak Greek as well as Roumanian; and they are all devoted members of the Greek Orthodox Church. Yet there has been a Roumanian propaganda in Macedonia since 1886, and the government at Bukarest has devoted large sums to the maintenance of Roumanian schools, of which the maximum number at any time has perhaps not exceeded forty.

Now if every other nation--Greek, Servian, Bulgarian--which had hitherto maintained its propaganda of schools and churches in Macedonia, was to bring its now emancipated children under the benign sway of the home government and also was to annex the Macedonian lands which they occupied, why, Roumania asked, should she be excluded from participation in the arrangement? She did not, it is true, join the Allies in fighting the common Moslem oppressor. But she maintained a benevolent neutrality. And since Macedonia is not conterminous with Roumania, she was not seeking to annex any portion of it. Yet the rights those Roumanians in Macedonia gave her should be satisfied. And so arguing, the Roumanian government claimed as a quid pro quo the adjoining northeastern corner of Bulgaria, permitting Bulgaria to recoup herself by the uncontested annexation of Thrace and Eastern Macedonia.

Such was the Roumanian reasoning. Certainly it bore hard on Bulgaria. But none of the belligerents showed any mercy on Bulgaria. War is a game of ruthless self-interest. It was Bulgaria who appealed to arms and she now had to pay the penalty. Her losses enriched all her neighbors. What Lord Bacon says of individuals is still more true of nations: the folly of one is the fortune of another, and none prospers so suddenly as by others' errors.

THE WORK AND REWARD OF MONTENEGRO

I have already sufficiently described the territorial gains of Roumania, Servia, and Greece. But I must not pass over Montenegro in silence. As the invincible warriors of King Nicholas opened the war against the Ottoman Empire, so they joined Servia and Greece in the struggle against Bulgaria. On Sunday, June 29, I saw encamped across the street from my hotel in Uskub 15,000 of these Montenegrin soldiers who had arrived only a day or two before by train from Mitrowitza, into which they had marched across Novi Bazar. Tall, lithe, daring, with countenances bespeaking clean lives, they looked as fine a body of men as one could find anywhere in the world, and their commanding figures and manly bearing were set off to great advantage by their striking and picturesque uniforms. The officers told me next day that in a few hours they would be fighting at Ghevgheli. Their splendid appearance seemed an augury of victory for the Serbs.

Montenegro too received her reward by an extension of territory on the south to the frontier of Albania (as fixed by the Great Powers) and a still more liberal extension on the east in the sandjak of Novi Bazar. This patriarchal kingdom will probably remain unchanged so long as the present King lives, the much-beloved King Nicholas, a genuinely Homeric Father of his People. But forces of an economic, social, and political character are already at work tending to draw it into closer union with Servia, and the Balkan wars have given a great impetus to these forces. A united Serb state, with an Adriatic littoral which would include the harbors of Antivari and Dulcigno, may be the future which destiny has in store for the sister kingdoms of Servia and Montenegro. If so, it is likely to be a mutually voluntary union; and neither Austria-Hungary nor Italy, the warders of the Adriatic, would seem to have any good ground to object to such a purely domestic arrangement.

THE PROBLEM OF ALBANIA

The Albanians, though they rather opposed than assisted the Allies in the war against Turkey, were set off as an independent nation by the Great Powers at the instigation of Austria-Hungary with the support of Italy. The determination of the boundaries of the new state was the resultant of conflicting forces in operation in the European concert. On the north while Scutari was retained for Albania through the insistence of Austria-Hungary, Russian influence was strong enough to secure the Albanian centres of Ipek and Djakova and Prisrend, as well as Dibra on the east, for the allied Serb states. This was a sort of compensation to Servia for her loss of an Adriatic outlet at a time when the war between the Allies, which was destined so greatly to extend her territories, was not foreseen. But while in this way Albanians were excluded from the new state on the north and east, an incongruous compensation was afforded it on the south by an unjustifiable extension into northern Epirus, whose population is prevailingly Greek.

The location of the boundary between Albania and New Greece was forced upon the Great Powers by the stand of Italy. During the first war the Greeks had occupied Epirus or southern Albania as far north as a line drawn from a point a little above Khimara on the coast due east toward Lake Presba, so that the cities of Tepeleni and Koritza were included in the Greek area. But Italy protested that the Greek occupation of territory on both sides of the Straits of Corfu would menace the control of the Adriatic and insisted that the boundary between Albania and Greece should start from a point on the coast opposite the southern part of the island of Corfu, Greece, accordingly, was compelled to evacuate most of the territory she had occupied above Janina. And Albania subsequently attempted to assert her jurisdiction over it.

But the task of Albania is bound to be difficult. For though the Great Powers have provided it with a ruler--the German Prince William of Wied--there is no organized state. The Albanians are one of the oldest races in Europe, if not the oldest. But they have never created a state. And to-day they are hopelessly divided. It is a land of universal opposition--north against south, tribe against tribe, bey against bey. The majority of the population are Mohammedan but there are many Roman Catholics in the north and in the south the Greek Orthodox Church is predominant. The inhabitants of the north, who are called Ghegs, are divided into numerous tribes whose principal occupation is fighting with one another under a system of perpetual blood-feuds and inextinguishable vendettas. There are no tribes in the south, but the people, who are known as Tosks, live under territorial magnates called beys, who are practically the absolute rulers of their districts. The country as a whole is a strange farrago of survivals of primitive conditions. And it is not only without art and literature, but without manufactures or trade or even agriculture. It is little wonder that the Greeks of Epirus feel outraged by the destiny which the European Powers have imposed upon them--to be torn from their own civilized and Christian kindred and subjected to the sway of the barbarous Mohammedans who occupy Albania. Nor is it surprising that since Hellenic armies have evacuated northern Epirus in conformity with the decree of the Great Powers, the inhabitants of the district, all the way from Santi Quaranta to Koritza, are declaring their independence and fighting the Albanians who attempt to bring them under the yoke.

The future of Albania is full of uncertainty. The State, however, was not created for the Albanians, who for the rest, are not in a condition to administer or maintain it. The state was established in the interests of Austria-Hungary and Italy. And those powers are likely to shape its future.

THE AEGEAN ISLANDS AND CRETE

For the sacrifice demanded of Greece in Epirus the Great Powers permitted her by way of compensation to retain all the Aegean Islands occupied by her during the war, except Imbros, Tenedos, and the Rabbit Islands at the mouth of the Dardanelles. These islands, however, Greece is never to fortify or convert into naval bases. This allotment of the Asiatic Islands (which includes all but Rhodes and the Dodecanese, temporarily held by Italy as a pledge of the evacuation of Libya by the Turkish officers and troops) has given great dissatisfaction in Turkey, where it is declared it would be better to have a war with Greece than cede certain islands especially Chios and Mitylene. The question of the disposition of the islands had, however, been committed by Turkey to the Great Powers in the Treaty of London. And Turkish unofficial condemnation of the action of the Powers now creates a dangerous situation. Mr. Venizelos declared not long ago, with the enthusiastic approval of the chamber, that the security of Greece lay alone in the possession of a strong navy. For Mr. Venizelos personally nothing in all these great events can have been more gratifying than the achievement of the union of Crete with Greece. This was consummated on December 14, when the Greek flag was hoisted on Canea Fort in the presence of King Constantine, the prime minister, and the consuls of the Great Powers, and saluted with 101 guns by the Greek fleet.

KING CONSTANTINE

Fortune in an extraordinary degree has favored the King of the Hellenes--Fortune and his own wise head and valiant arm and the loyal support of his people. When before has a Prince taken supreme command of a nation's army and in the few months preceding and succeeding his accession to the throne by successful generalship doubled the area and population of his country?

COST OF THE WAR

The Balkan wars have been bloody and costly. We shall never know of the thousands of men, women, and children who died from privation, disease, and massacre. But the losses of the dead and wounded in the armies were for Montenegro 11,200, for Greece 68,000, for Servia 71,000, for Bulgaria 156,000, and for Turkey about the same as for Bulgaria. The losses in treasure were as colossal as in blood. Only rough computations are possible. But the direct military expenditures are estimated at figures varying from a billion and a quarter to a billion and a half of dollars. This of course takes no account of the paralysis of productive industry, trade, and commerce or of the destruction of existing economic values.

Yet great and momentous results have been achieved. Although seated again in his ancient capital of Adrianople, the Moslem has been expelled from Europe, or at any rate is no longer a European Power. For the first time in more than five centuries, therefore, conditions of stable equilibrium are now possible for the Christian nations of the Balkans. Whether the present alignment of those states toward one another and towards the Great Powers is destined to continue it would be foolhardy to attempt to predict.

THE FUTURE OF THE BALKANS

But without pretending to cast a horoscope, certain significant facts may be mentioned in a concluding word. If the Balkan states are left to themselves, if they are permitted to settle their own affairs without the intervention of the Great Powers, there is no reason why the existing relations between Greece, Servia, Montenegro, and Roumania, founded as they are on mutual interest, should not continue; and if they continue, peace will be assured in spite of Bulgaria's cry for revenge and readjustment. The danger lies in the influence of the Great Powers with their varying attractions and repulsions. France, Germany, and Great Britain, disconnected with the Balkans and remote from them, are not likely to exert much direct individual influence. But their connections with the Triple Alliance and the Triple Entente would not leave them altogether free to take isolated action. And two other members of those European groups--Russia and Austria-Hungary--have long been vitally interested in the Balkan question; while the opposition to Servian annexation on the Adriatic littoral and of Greek annexation in Epirus now for the first time reveals the deep concern of Italy in the same question.

The Serbs are Slavs. And the unhappy relations between Servia and Austria-Hungary have always intensified their pro-Russian proclivities. The Roumanians are a Romance people, like the French and Italians, and they have hitherto been regarded as a Balkan extension of the Triple Alliance. The attitude of Austria-Hungary, however, during the Balkan wars has caused a cooling of Roumanian friendship, so that its transference to Russia is no longer inconceivable or even improbable. Greece desires to be independent of both groups of the European system, but the action of Italy in regard to Northern Epirus and in regard to Rhodes and the Dodecanese has produced a feeling of irritation and resentment among the Greeks which nothing is likely to allay or even greatly alleviate. Bulgaria in the past has carried her desire to live an independent national life to the point of hostility to Russia, but since Stambuloff's time she has shown more natural sentiments towards her great Slav sister and liberator. Whether the desire of revenge against Servia (and Greece) will once more draw her toward Austria-Hungary only time can disclose.

In any event it will take a long time for all the Balkan states to recover from the terrible exhaustion of the two wars of 1912 and 1913.

Their financial resources have been depleted; their male population has been decimated. Necessity, therefore, is likely to co-operate with the community of interest established by the Treaty of Bukarest in the maintenance of conditions of stable equilibrium in the Balkans. Of course the peace-compelling forces operative in the Balkan states themselves might be counteracted by hostile activities on the part of some of the Great Powers. And there is one danger-point for which the Great Powers themselves are solely responsible. This, as I have already explained, is Albania. An artificial creation with unnatural boundaries, it is a grave question whether this so-called state can either manage its own affairs or live in peace with its Serb and Greek neighbors. At this moment the Greeks of Epirus (whom the Great Powers have transferred to Albania) are resisting to the death incorporation in a state which outrages their deepest and holiest sentiments of religion, race, nationality, and humane civilization. On the other hand the Hoti and Gruda tribes on the north fiercely resent annexation to Montenegro (which the Great Powers have decreed) and threaten to summon to their support other Malissori tribes with whom they have had a defensive alliance for several centuries. If Prince William of Wied is unable to cope with these difficulties, Italy and Austria-Hungary may think it necessary to intervene in Albania. But the intervention of either would almost certainly provoke compensatory action on the part of other European Powers, especially Russia.

One can only hope that the Great Powers may have wisdom granted to them to find a peaceful solution of the embarrassing problem which they have created in setting up the new state of Albania. That the Albanians themselves will have an opportunity to develop their own national independence I find it impossible to believe. Yet I heard in the summer of 1913 at Valona from the lips of Ismail Kemal Bey, the head of the provisional government, a most impressive statement of his hopes and aspirations for an independent Albania and his faith and confidence in its future, in which he claimed to voice the sentiments of the Albanian people. But, as I have already explained, I think it doubtful whether under the most favorable external circumstances the Albanians are at present qualified to establish and maintain an independent state. And their destiny is so inextricably entangled with the ambitions of some of the Great Powers that the experiment stands no chance of getting a fair trial. I heartily wish the circumstances were other than they are. For as an American I sympathize with the aspirations of all struggling nationalities to be free and independent. And my interest in Albania is deepened, as the interest of all Americans must be deepened, by the fact that a large number of Albanians have now found a home in the United States.

www.bookjungle.com *email: sales@bookjungle.com fax: 630-214-0564 mail: Book Jungle PO Box 2226 Champaign, IL 61825*

The Codes Of Hammurabi And Moses
W. W. Davies

QTY

The discovery of the Hammurabi Code is one of the greatest achievements of archaeology, and is of paramount interest, not only to the student of the Bible, but also to all those interested in ancient history...

Religion ISBN: *1-59462-338-4* Pages:132
MSRP $12.95

The Theory of Moral Sentiments
Adam Smith

QTY

This work from 1749. contains original theories of conscience amd moral judgment and it is the foundation for systemof morals.

Philosophy ISBN: *1-59462-777-0* Pages:536
MSRP $19.95

Jessica's First Prayer
Hesba Stretton

QTY

In a screened and secluded corner of one of the many railway-bridges which span the streets of London there could be seen a few years ago, from five o'clock every morning until half past eight, a tidily set-out coffee-stall, consisting of a trestle and board, upon which stood two large tin cans, with a small fire of charcoal burning under each so as to keep the coffee boiling during the early hours of the morning when the work-people were thronging into the city on their way to their daily toil...

Childrens ISBN: *1-59462-373-2* Pages:84
MSRP $9.95

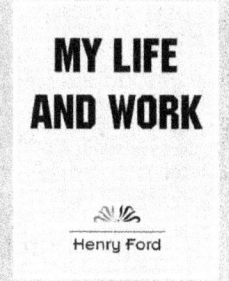

My Life and Work
Henry Ford

QTY

Henry Ford revolutionized the world with his implementation of mass production for the Model T automobile. Gain valuable business insight into his life and work with his own auto-biography... "We have only started on our development of our country we have not as yet, with all our talk of wonderful progress, done more than scratch the surface. The progress has been wonderful enough but..."

Biographies/ ISBN: *1-59462-198-5* Pages:300
MSRP $21.95

www.bookjungle.com *email: sales@bookjungle.com fax: 630-214-0564 mail: Book Jungle PO Box 2226 Champaign, IL 61825*

The Art of Cross-Examination
Francis Wellman

QTY

I presume it is the experience of every author, after his first book is published upon an important subject, to be almost overwhelmed with a wealth of ideas and illustrations which could readily have been included in his book, and which to his own mind, at least, seem to make a second edition inevitable. Such certainly was the case with me; and when the first edition had reached its sixth impression in five months, I rejoiced to learn that it seemed to my publishers that the book had met with a sufficiently favorable reception to justify a second and considerably enlarged edition. ..

Reference   ISBN: *1-59462-647-2*   Pages:412   MSRP *$19.95*

On the Duty of Civil Disobedience
Henry David Thoreau

QTY

Thoreau wrote his famous essay, On the Duty of Civil Disobedience, as a protest against an unjust but popular war and the immoral but popular institution of slave-owning. He did more than write—he declined to pay his taxes, and was hauled off to gaol in consequence. Who can say how much this refusal of his hastened the end of the war and of slavery ?

Law   ISBN: *1-59462-747-9*   Pages:48   MSRP *$7.45*

Dream Psychology Psychoanalysis for Beginners
Sigmund Freud

QTY

Sigmund Freud, born Sigismund Schlomo Freud (May 6, 1856 - September 23, 1939), was a Jewish-Austrian neurologist and psychiatrist who co-founded the psychoanalytic school of psychology. Freud is best known for his theories of the unconscious mind, especially involving the mechanism of repression; his redefinition of sexual desire as mobile and directed towards a wide variety of objects; and his therapeutic techniques, especially his understanding of transference in the therapeutic relationship and the presumed value of dreams as sources of insight into unconscious desires.

Psychology   ISBN: *1-59462-905-6*   Pages:196   MSRP *$15.45*

The Miracle of Right Thought
Orison Swett Marden

QTY

Believe with all of your heart that you will do what you were made to do. When the mind has once formed the habit of holding cheerful, happy, prosperous pictures, it will not be easy to form the opposite habit. It does not matter how improbable or how far away this realization may see, or how dark the prospects may be, if we visualize them as best we can, as vividly as possible, hold tenaciously to them and vigorously struggle to attain them, they will gradually become actualized, realized in the life. But a desire, a longing without endeavor, a yearning abandoned or held indifferently will vanish without realization.

Self Help   ISBN: *1-59462-644-8*   Pages:360   MSRP *$25.45*

www.bookjungle.com email: sales@bookjungle.com fax: 630-214-0564 mail: Book Jungle PO Box 2226 Champaign, IL 61825

QTY

	Title	ISBN	Price
☐	**The Rosicrucian Cosmo-Conception Mystic Christianity** by *Max Heindel* The Rosicrucian Cosmo-conception is not dogmatic, neither does it appeal to any other authority than the reason of the student. It is: not controversial, but is: sent forth in the, hope that it may help to clear...	ISBN: 1-59462-188-8 New Age/Religion Pages 646	$38.95
☐	**Abandonment To Divine Providence** by *Jean-Pierre de Caussade* "The Rev. Jean Pierre de Caussade was one of the most remarkable spiritual writers of the Society of Jesus in France in the 18th Century. His death took place at Toulouse in 1751. His works have gone through many editions and have been republished...	ISBN: 1-59462-228-0 Inspirational/Religion Pages 400	$25.95
☐	**Mental Chemistry** by *Charles Haanel* Mental Chemistry allows the change of material conditions by combining and appropriately utilizing the power of the mind. Much like applied chemistry creates something new and unique out of careful combinations of chemicals the mastery of mental chemistry...	ISBN: 1-59462-192-6 New Age Pages 354	$23.95
☐	**The Letters of Robert Browning and Elizabeth Barret Barrett 1845-1846 vol II** by *Robert Browning and Elizabeth Barrett*	ISBN: 1-59462-193-4 Biographies Pages 596	$35.95
☐	**Gleanings In Genesis (volume I)** by *Arthur W. Pink* Appropriately has Genesis been termed "the seed plot of the Bible" for in it we have, in germ form, almost all of the great doctrines which are afterwards fully developed in the books of Scripture which follow...	ISBN: 1-59462-130-6 Religion/Inspirational Pages 420	$27.45
☐	**The Master Key** by *L. W. de Laurence* In no branch of human knowledge has there been a more lively increase of the spirit of research during the past few years than in the study of Psychology, Concentration and Mental Discipline. The requests for authentic lessons in Thought Control, Mental Discipline and...	ISBN: 1-59462-001-6 New Age/Business Pages 422	$30.95
☐	**The Lesser Key Of Solomon Goetia** by *L. W. de Laurence* This translation of the first book of the "Lemegton" which is for the first time made accessible to students of Talismanic Magic was done, after careful collation and edition, from numerous Ancient Manuscripts in Hebrew, Latin, and French...	ISBN: 1-59462-092-X New Age/Occult Pages 92	$9.95
☐	**Rubaiyat Of Omar Khayyam** by *Edward Fitzgerald* Edward Fitzgerald, whom the world has already learned, in spite of his own efforts to remain within the shadow of anonymity, to look upon as one of the rarest poets of the century, was born at Bredfield, in Suffolk, on the 31st of March, 1809. He was the third son of John Purcell...	ISBN:1-59462-332-5 Music Pages 172	$13.95
☐	**Ancient Law** by *Henry Maine* The chief object of the following pages is to indicate some of the earliest ideas of mankind, as they are reflected in Ancient Law, and to point out the relation of those ideas to modern thought.	ISBN: 1-59462-128-4 Religiom/History Pages 452	$29.95
☐	**Far-Away Stories** by *William J. Locke* "Good wine needs no bush, but a collection of mixed vintages does. And this book is just such a collection. Some of the stories I do not want to remain buried for ever in the museum files of dead magazine-numbers an author's not unpardonable vanity..."	ISBN: 1-59462-129-2 Fiction Pages 272	$19.45
☐	**Life of David Crockett** by *David Crockett* "Colonel David Crockett was one of the most remarkable men of the times in which he lived. Born in humble life, but gifted with a strong will, an indomitable courage, and unremitting perseverance...	ISBN: 1-59462-250-7 Biographies/New Age Pages 424	$27.45
☐	**Lip-Reading** by *Edward Nitchie* Edward B. Nitchie, founder of the New York School for the Hard of Hearing, now the Nitchie School of Lip-Reading, Inc, wrote "LIP-READING Principles and Practice". The development and perfecting of this meritorious work on lip-reading was an undertaking...	ISBN: 1-59462-206-X How-to Pages 400	$25.95
☐	**A Handbook of Suggestive Therapeutics, Applied Hypnotism, Psychic Science** by *Henry Munro*	ISBN: 1-59462-214-0 Health/New Age/Health/Self-help Pages 376	$24.95
☐	**A Doll's House: and Two Other Plays** by *Henrik Ibsen* Henrik Ibsen created this classic when in revolutionary 1848 Rome. Introducing some striking concepts in playwriting for the realist genre, this play has been studied the world over.	ISBN: 1-59462-112-8 Fiction/Classics/Plays 308	$19.95
☐	**The Light of Asia** by *sir Edwin Arnold* In this poetic masterpiece, Edwin Arnold describes the life and teachings of Buddha. The man who was to become known as Buddha to the world was born as Prince Gautama of India but he rejected the worldly riches and abandoned the reigns of power when...	ISBN: 1-59462-204-3 Religion/History/Biographies Pages 170	$13.95
☐	**The Complete Works of Guy de Maupassant** by *Guy de Maupassant* "For days and days, nights and nights, I had dreamed of that first kiss which was to consecrate our engagement, and I knew not on what spot I should put my lips..."	ISBN: 1-59462-157-8 Fiction/Classics Pages 240	$16.95
☐	**The Art of Cross-Examination** by *Francis L. Wellman* Written by a renowned trial lawyer, Wellman imparts his experience and uses case studies to explain how to use psychology to extract desired information through questioning.	ISBN: 1-59462-309-0 How-to/Science/Reference Pages 408	$26.95
☐	**Answered or Unanswered?** by *Louisa Vaughan* Miracles of Faith in China	ISBN: 1-59462-248-5 Religion Pages 112	$10.95
☐	**The Edinburgh Lectures on Mental Science (1909)** by *Thomas* This book contains the substance of a course of lectures recently given by the writer in the Queen Street Hall, Edinburgh. Its purpose is to indicate the Natural Principles governing the relation between Mental Action and Material Conditions...	ISBN: 1-59462-008-3 New Age/Psychology Pages 148	$11.95
☐	**Ayesha** by *H. Rider Haggard* Verily and indeed it is the unexpected that happens! Probably if there was one person upon the earth from whom the Editor of this, and of a certain previous history, did not expect to hear again...	ISBN: 1-59462-301-5 Classics Pages 380	$24.95
☐	**Ayala's Angel** by *Anthony Trollope* The two girls were both pretty, but Lucy who was twenty-one who supposed to be simple and comparatively unattractive, whereas Ayala was credited, as her Bombwhat romantic name might show, with poetic charm and a taste for romance. Ayala when her father died was nineteen...	ISBN: 1-59462-352-X Fiction Pages 484	$29.95
☐	**The American Commonwealth** by *James Bryce* An interpretation of American democratic political theory. It examines political mechanics and society from the perspective of Scotsman James Bryce	ISBN: 1-59462-286-8 Politics Pages 572	$34.45
☐	**Stories of the Pilgrims** by *Margaret P. Pumphrey* This book explores pilgrims religious oppression in England as well as their escape to Holland and eventual crossing to America on the Mayflower, and their early days in New England...	ISBN: 1-59462-116-0 History Pages 268	$17.95

www.bookjungle.com email: sales@bookjungle.com fax: 630-214-0564 mail: Book Jungle PO Box 2226 Champaign, IL 61825

QTY

The Fasting Cure *by Sinclair Upton*   ISBN: *1-59462-222-1* $13.95
In the Cosmopolitan Magazine for May, 1910, and in the Contemporary Review (London) for April, 1910, I published an article dealing with my experiences in fasting. I have written a great many magazine articles, but never one which attracted so much attention...   *New Age/Self Help/Health Pages 164*

Hebrew Astrology *by Sepharial*   ISBN: *1-59462-308-2* $13.45
In these days of advanced thinking it is a matter of common observation that we have left many of the old landmarks behind and that we are now pressing forward to greater heights and to a wider horizon than that which represented the mind-content of our progenitors...   *Astrology Pages 144*

Thought Vibration or The Law of Attraction in the Thought World   ISBN: *1-59462-127-6* $12.95
by William Walker Atkinson   *Psychology/Religion Pages 144*

Optimism *by Helen Keller*   ISBN: *1-59462-108-X* $15.95
Helen Keller was blind, deaf, and mute since 19 months old, yet famously learned how to overcome these handicaps, communicate with the world, and spread her lectures promoting optimism. An inspiring read for everyone...   *Biographies/Inspirational Pages 84*

Sara Crewe *by Frances Burnett*   ISBN: *1-59462-360-0* $9.45
In the first place, Miss Minchin lived in London. Her home was a large, dull, tall one, in a large, dull square, where all the houses were alike, and all the sparrows were alike, and where all the door-knockers made the same heavy sound...   *Childrens/Classic Pages 88*

The Autobiography of Benjamin Franklin *by Benjamin Franklin*   ISBN: *1-59462-135-7* $24.95
The Autobiography of Benjamin Franklin has probably been more extensively read than any other American historical work, and no other book of its kind has had such ups and downs of fortune. Franklin lived for many years in England, where he was agent...   *Biographies/History Pages 332*

Name	
Email	
Telephone	
Address	
City, State ZIP	

☐ Credit Card   ☐ Check / Money Order

Credit Card Number	
Expiration Date	
Signature	

Please Mail to: Book Jungle
                    PO Box 2226
                    Champaign, IL 61825
or Fax to: 630-214-0564

ORDERING INFORMATION

web: *www.bookjungle.com*
email: *sales@bookjungle.com*
fax: *630-214-0564*
mail: *Book Jungle PO Box 2226 Champaign, IL 61825*
or PayPal *to sales@bookjungle.com*

Please contact us for bulk discounts

DIRECT-ORDER TERMS

**20% Discount if You Order
Two or More Books**
Free Domestic Shipping!
Accepted: Master Card, Visa,
Discover, American Express

www.ingramcontent.com/pod-product-compliance
Lightning Source LLC
Chambersburg PA
CBHW081327040426
42453CB00013B/2320